Seven Virtues for Success

Seven Virtues for Success

GEORGE TSAKIRIDIS

WIPF & STOCK · Eugene, Oregon

SEVEN VIRTUES FOR SUCCESS

Wipf & Stock
An Imprint of Wipf and Stock Publishers
199 W. 8th Ave., Suite 3
Eugene, OR 97401

www.wipfandstock.com

PAPERBACK ISBN: 978-1-6667-3021-0
HARDCOVER ISBN: 978-1-6667-2142-3
EBOOK ISBN: 978-1-6667-2143-0

12/09/21

To Jocelyn
With Love

Contents

Preface

THIS BOOK IS THE culmination of ten or so years of thinking about virtue in my own life. I began with three base virtues—humility, gratitude, and diligence—perhaps mirroring the Franciscan trio of poverty, chastity, and obedience in a quick way to repeat the virtues important to me. From there it grew over time, finishing with the seven you see in this book. I suspect I am not done. Living a virtuous life is always a work in progress, and I am no exception. Virtue is something we continually strive for, yet fail in doing. My goal in sharing this text with you is to prompt you to think about core virtues that can help your own life. The way you practice them may differ from person to person, but the virtues themselves seem to be at the base of living a successful life. Whether that be spiritually, emotionally, or in your vocation, building good character through virtue is essential. Using cognitive reinforcement, we can continually re-center ourselves in the virtues we hold dear. In this way we are building a habit of excellent character.

Just like the text itself, I have kept this preface brief. Though I believe the implementation of virtue is quite difficult, the core principles are very simple. I trust you find this book helpful. Even if it just gets you thinking about the way your character has and will develop, it will have been a success.

Introduction

C AN I LET YOU in on a little secret? Life is difficult. Don't get me wrong, life is great, fulfilling, and full of beauty. But it *is* difficult. If you look back over your lifetime, you might find that you can start listing tragic events in the world that you forgot happened. Whether they be on a personal level, a community level, or a global one, this might be quite the laundry list. It might be a death; it might be a war; it might be lost love. Struggle is a part of life. This is not necessarily a bad thing. We all handle these events in different ways. The following pages contain my thoughts on navigating this difficulty in our day-to-day lives.

Like some of you, I am a competitive, driven person. This creates a lot of advantages in life, but also a lot of difficulties. Personally, I care that things are fair, just, and good. And I want to create fairness as much as I am able, but life doesn't always work out like that. Sometimes we have to accept injustice as a part of life, knowing that justice will come later. I am also an optimist. And ultimately to change your own life, character, and trajectory, you must be optimistic. You must believe that things can be changed. Sometimes it is hard to be optimistic, and you may be feeling that right now. Recently, the world has experienced the COVID-19 pandemic. Whatever one thinks of the decisions made and the dangers connected to this virus, we can all agree that it has had a major effect on the world. I mention this, because though this book is not specifically about the pandemic, it was the final catalyst for me in writing this text. Whatever struggle is currently on your mind, I hope that this text helps you reset and renews your optimism to take a necessary path forward.

In this vein, I had already been working on a book that dealt with virtues and our lives. Let me explain. My academic career did not get off to the rosy start that I anticipated. Nowadays few do. Up to that point, I was often the youngest, the brightest, and the one with promise. I entered academia mildly hopeful that this would continue. I trusted I would receive my due. What I found is that, just like many of us find in life, what is fair, expected, or both, is not always what comes to fruition. The pandemic has solidified and furthered my thoughts on virtue and faith exponentially, and prompted me to write this text. It was through my earlier frustration that I came to the conclusion that humility, gratitude, and diligence were the cardinal virtues for succeeding in life. I later added forgiveness to this list. Subsequently, I've added others, and this book is the culmination of that list. My intention is to spend a chapter on each of the chosen virtues, ponder them, and present a path forward for times of both difficulty and plenty.

Difficult times need not be a waste of years for those of us with ambition, but a time of rest, strengthening, and a fresh start. When our expectations are no longer possible, we are freed to commit to the reality of doing our best in what is actual versus what we perceive as actual. This is ultimately an issue of justice, an issue of fairness. At its most charitable reading, we are frustrated and angry because life is not fair. Times of extreme difficulty force us to accept this reality. Life is not *fair*. It is not *just*. Acceptance of these truths opens up the possibility for the enjoyment of life because we are no longer beholden to the utopia we think should exist, but are forced to make our way in the reality that does exist. This starts with humility.

Humility is the point at which we realize our own limitations, and defer to a higher power. A simple definition states that humility is dealing with reality as it is, and not as we wish it to be. This is what catastrophic events force us to do. If you do not accept humility, there will come a point at which it is forced upon you. Following from humility is gratitude. *Gratitude* emerges from humility because once we accept our place in the order of the universe, we respond with thankfulness for what we do have, realizing that many do not have these same things. This drives us toward *diligence*, which is the hard work we must put in out of obligation to our humanity, but also in order to achieve the things we now know are valuable to us, based on a reflection of our situation. Through this, our diligence is refocused on what matters, not on uncontrolled expectations. Our humility leads us to realize that more must be done in order to achieve the things we think important, whether this be in the spiritual realm or the physical one. We shouldn't stop at the point we think we have done enough, but only when the goal is realized. Then we should focus our diligence toward the next goal.

Further, *agency* is tied to diligence, realizing what we can and cannot control. Our agency is freed to work on the things that are essential to us, as our will is freed. Paralleling these virtues of diligence and agency are those of *relationship* and *forgiveness*. Based on our humility and gratitude we are now able to see how relationship is important to our lives and also gives us the perspective to forgive both others and ourselves. This emerges from the grounding we experience in God's love and divinity. As relationships are put on hold or destroyed through something like the pandemic we just experienced, it forces us to realize the importance (or unimportance) of those relationships. This is true in both the virtual world of social media and the "real" world. This may especially be seen in our relationships at our places of worship and with God.

Lastly, *kindness* emerges as an action that we can take to encourage, restore, and strengthen relationships with our family, friends, and even acquaintances and strangers. Kindness is the last step. And that kindness is centered in love.

We can think of these virtues as divided into three "A's: first the virtues of *awareness* (humility and gratitude), then the virtues of *action* (diligence and agency), finishing with the virtues of *agreement* (relationship, forgiveness, and kindness). Not only does it give us a catchy AAA acronym to remember these virtues and divide them up neatly, it also shows progression in the virtuous path from internal (awareness) to external—self (action) to external—community (agreement), where these virtues can reach fulfillment on a broader scale.

Of course, there are other virtues that are a part of this recentering. Honesty and character come to mind. These are at the core of a virtuous person. But allow me to discuss them within the context of our seven virtues. Honesty and good character should already be present in the person reading this text. And specifically humility, gratitude, and forgiveness spring from this virtue of honesty, which allows our authentic self to blossom and grow.

The concept of good character is a general idea that involves intention and a combination of virtues. If you are reading this with the intention of making your character better, you are already on the path to virtue. You still must enact it, but you are on the path. Honesty is more pertinent to our discussion.

To put it in terms of our journey, let us call honesty the previrtue. You must be honest in order to be virtuous. Think about where all the good virtues in life come from. Think about what is at their root—honesty. Without honesty, you will not be humble. Without honesty, you will not be grateful. Without honesty, you will not forgive or be kind. Because virtue requires honesty. How can I be truly kind to someone without being honest with who I am and who they are? I can be "nice," but to be virtuous, I must be truthful about who I am in the light of God and humanity, and who they are in that same light. This will drive me to virtue. Those who lie to self, others, or God will find themselves struggling to commit to the fullness of the virtues described in this text. I know this from my own experience, and I suspect you do also. I don't mean that I tell outright lies. I mean that sometimes we are not openly honest with ourselves about who we are, and who others are, and who God is. Truthfulness is the starting point for all of us. If you can be honest, you can continue the path of virtue. And contrary to some misconceptions, honesty does not mean being cruel or blunt in a way that is weaponized. It means telling the truth in love—to yourself, to others, and to God. This is the gateway to the rest of this path. With this always in mind, let us start walking that path.

Before I get to the principal seven virtues, let me share the three main things that I've learned from difficult circumstances. *First, we must accept that things are out of our control.* The façade of control is one that we continually strive for and protect. When we cannot control large things, we look to control minutia, which can manifest itself as unhealthy psychological behaviors. Through difficult life events, we are forced to realize how much is truly out of our control. How many people lost their jobs, loved ones, or even their life to a situation that was unexpected like a natural disaster, a pandemic, or a war? This brings us to the question that many throughout history have used as an excuse to lose their faith in God: Why do people suffer? Why do bad things happen to "good" people? These questions are difficult to answer, but become much easier when one accepts that what "should" happen is not always the reality of what does happen. Be this to sin or an evolutionary process that thrives on suffering, the reality is that people see themselves as better than they are—more deserving than they are. It is this lie that many of us believe that leads to such dissatisfaction with life and faith.[1]

Second, we must be grateful for the things we do have. This second maxim spawns the list of virtues I previously mentioned. When you know that all is out of your control, it is then that you can accept what is given to you and cherish it. As should be clear from the previous list of virtues, this is not to encourage laziness, but to re-center our focus on being diligent for the things we know are imperative to both ourselves, our community, and ultimately God, who should be reflected in the former two. Gratitude leads to more diligent, meaningful work, and also more happiness. When one is not grateful they start to accept that they are entitled to what they have, and this expectation leads to sloth, which leads to less

---

1. This does not mean we shouldn't strive for good things or work for achievement. In fact, it is the opposite; it enforces the fact that we must work toward our goals. Accomplishment is not typically handed to us because we "deserve" it.

reward, which continues a spiral downward. Gratitude is not saying that what one has or experiences is up to chance, but states that there should be thankfulness to God and others for those things.

Third, when faced with a new reality, expectations change. We are no longer expected to finish the projects we once did. We are no longer expected to be in touch with friends as we once were. This lack of expectation frees us to truly follow the work we want to do and connect with the people we want to be with. When expectations drop, we are freed to be our true selves. Our expectations for relationships change. We realize how empty virtual relationships truly are. Social networks and virtual meetings are useful, and in conjunction with "real" relationships they can be valuable. But alone, they are a shadow of the connection we are meant to have as human beings. I am reminded of the work of Albert Borgmann and Hubert Dreyfus who discuss virtual relationships as being less than whole relationships.[2] The virtual relationships to which we cling are helpful, yet also mirror a lack of true fulfillment. Often, we try to meet social expectations in a misguided search for love and relationship. When this false love goes away it points us back to true relationship. Why continue this façade for something so clearly false? A new paradigm can have the effect of revealing the true nature of these false expectations.

This book is laid out as a series of chapters, starting in chapter 1 by ruminating on these three lessons. I will then spend a chapter discussing virtue in a historical sense, followed by seven chapters, each one dedicated to the virtues that are cardinal in this context: humility, gratitude, diligence, agency, relationship, forgiveness, and kindness (love). This text is not an academic text or a strictly self-help book. It is meant to highlight those thoughts that I feel are important in the midst of the difficulties we face in our lives. It is a record of my own thoughts that have been building over the past several years and have been recently crystalized. It is a meditation, a rumination, a look at the internal thoughts of someone who has both studied these things, and (attempted to) live them.

2. "Social Networking and Ethics."

Introduction

The virtues and maxims found in this book also have another side, a darker side. I would not know forgiveness if I did not know guilt. I would not know love if I did not know hatred. I would not know diligence if I did not know sloth. These concepts will find their way into the pages of this book, and are a necessary part of the formation of virtue. Humans often know virtue through their experience of vice. To put this in terms of Christianity, the radical nature of the salvation offered in Jesus Christ is only powerful in light of a powerful evil that must be overcome. If we do not know sin, we cannot know salvation. What is there to be saved from if we are not in danger in the first place? This is where many theologies go wrong. They attempt to minimize the evil of the world, and in the process they minimize the need for powerful good. In times of suffering, we are forced to look at a situation that reflects our shortcomings. It puts us under a microscope in which we now must take responsibility for our decisions (*agency*). To know virtue is to know vice. To do what is good requires that we know what is evil. The struggles of life give us an opportunity to throw aside the expectations that hide mediocrity and glorified evil, and renew and strengthen our character. With this renewal, we can do the things we have been called to do in this life.

1

Three Things I Learned in Difficulty

A s I mentioned in the previous chapter, there are three things that I have learned, or better said, relearned, in difficult circumstances. First, we must accept that things are out of our control. Second, we must be grateful for the things we have. Third, when faced with a new reality, expectations change, including relationship expectations. In this chapter, I'm going to muse on these three, especially the third, before moving on to the virtues. There are plenty of other lessons, but those can come out organically through the discussion of virtue and our response to difficult times.

First, *we must accept things that are out of our control.* This means you. This also means me. This is one of the most difficult things for me to accept. It is a continual power play. What happens is that an event takes place in your life that forces you to become humble, to accept what you have no choice but to accept. In response, you have a short-term realization that you are not in control. Usually this will be followed by an attempt to gain control in some other aspect of your life, whether large or small. It could be as simple as ordering lunch because eating out will make you feel better. These temporary salves make us feel better for a short time, but never deal with the underlying problem, which is dissatisfaction with our circumstances. In our dissatisfaction, we look for satisfaction. The problem is, for many of us, we look for short-term fulfillment and miss the larger need.

However, in a paradigm-shifting event, we are continually reminded of our circumstances. We have limitations placed on our freedom, and some of those short-term fixes are no longer available to us. For example, when the pandemic first broke, eating out for lunch was no longer available to me as a viable option. So that coping mechanism was taken away, pointing me back to my circumstances. I might then be forced to deal with the actual root of my dissatisfaction because my "cheap" coping mechanism was removed. Lack of control helps us see things as they really are. It removes false hope, and, if we're paying attention, it points us to actual solutions for our difficulties. Some of these challenges emerge from unfounded dissatisfaction, while others come from a real need that we have to address. A drastic change in circumstances helps to make this more apparent.

Furthering this theme, one of the greatest evils of our time is materialism. Both people of faith, and, funny enough, scientific materialists, can agree that the lust for possessions is harmful to one's "soul." In times where we are forced to be apart, be it for health reasons or a major crisis in the world, we are pushed away from material things because one of the major impetuses for them is gone—that of boasting. When we buy things, one of our intentions is to show them to others to gain their approval. If we cannot show off our wares, we no longer take joy in flaunting them. If funds are needed for survival, there is a smaller amount of money left to feed our lesser impulses.

But there's another side to this. If we don't keep our agency in the midst of difficulty, we will be pulled along by a sense of being adrift. Accepting we do not control everything does not mean allowing the winds of life to take us wherever they will. It means knowing our limitations and working within them. Pushing those boundaries is valuable, but knowing that there are boundaries gives us structure. It lets us know that we cannot do everything, and abrogates our responsibility to do so. It is an interesting balance: the optimism and motivation to try things, to do what we want, checked by the knowledge that we cannot do everything. Thus, even in accepting our limits, we embrace our agency. It is not a resignation that all is decided for us, it is a robust knowledge of what is possible. It is a freedom given once knowledge is embraced.

Let me put this another way. I believe strongly in setting goals and executing those goals. The path to do so is not always direct. In fact, it rarely is. When catastrophic events get in our way, they force us to review those goals. Are they possible? What must yet be done to achieve them? But most importantly, are they really the goals you want to achieve? Major events force us to reevaluate what we've been spending our time on. Extreme times of trial create an opportunity to drop misguided goals without the pressure of societal expectation that comes with leaving behind those goals. It connects directly back to the concept of materialism. If our desires are set with the focus of impressing others, but are not our own desires, they should be abandoned. Difficult circumstances show us that time is limited: that we cannot control everything we thought we could. We must embrace this limitation, and in the cognitive knowledge of embracing limitation, we are emancipated from our prison of ill-advised expectations. Far from being prevented from achieving our purpose, we are liberated to seek it because the idol of false ambitions has been tarnished and presented as the faux god it truly is.

Which brings us to . . .

We must be grateful for the things we do have. If we've torn down the idol of false ambitions, we can look around and see things as they truly are. With this new sight, we find ourselves grateful for the things we have, for the situation we are in, for the people we have relationships with, and for the God we know and love.

Gratitude is not acceptance of the status quo. It is not deluding yourself into being happy with where you are for the rest of your life. However, it is being thankful and appreciative for where you are right now. This might include being thankful for things in your past or things yet to come. It might be looking for blessings to be thankful for in the midst of struggle. There are a couple things that emerge from this attitude. *First,* you create a mindset that focuses on the positive, which begets more positive thoughts and actions. *Second,* you center yourself in your actuality versus what you think should be actual.

To the first point, creating a mindset that focuses on positive things in your life seemingly begets more joy, more thankfulness, and more of the things you might complain you are missing otherwise. So, funny enough, the thing that pushes us forward is the thing that is antithetical to a mindset of pushing forward. Let me explain, as this is something I have struggled with a lot in my own life. If you are a practitioner of some of the Chinese internal martial arts, Tai Chi, for instance, you will notice that when you firm up and push or attack by forcing something where it does not belong, you end up harming yourself. Going with the flow of energy and redirecting that energy is what allows you to create maximum force on an opponent. In internal martial arts, *intent* is paramount, but the way that intent is directed is also critical. In the same way, when we push our desires and our goals in a direction that is not maximizing our humility, our gratitude, or any other one of many virtues, we are not going to be as successful as we would otherwise. Just as in the Chinese marital arts, you want to follow the natural way of virtue as opposed to fighting what is good in an attempt to force desires.

As I define it, gratitude does not mean accepting one's station in life without the hope of more. However, it does mean being thankful for one's place in life at the moment you are experiencing it. Think about it this way: if you are thirty years old, you might think "I am nowhere near where I should be in my career/love life/psychological well-being at this point in my life. I am a failure." This could be done at any age. If you do not step back from where you are and become grateful for what you have and what you have accomplished, you will not move forward. By focusing on the good in your life, you can then build on that good and use where you are currently in order to reach that future goal. This is true in both the material and the spiritual world. When we try to force satisfaction, or dissatisfaction, upon ourselves, we will always be disappointed because internally we know this to be a lie. By focusing on thankfulness and gratitude, we accept the truth, and the satisfaction that comes with it. This allows us to move forward. You may not like where you are at age thirty, but if you continue that dissatisfaction, you will not like where you are at age forty or fifty either. You will have regrets, and will have accomplished nothing. Turn to gratitude with a healthy dose of hope and reality, and you will pivot forward.

With an eye to the Christian Scriptures, there's a good reason the book of Galatians tells us that the fruit of the spirit is love, joy, peace, etc. You bear positive fruit when your spirit is right. This manifests itself most fully in relationship with Jesus Christ, but the principles apply to all who are grateful. This is borne out by both scientific experiment and the spiritual life in many traditions.

Further, to my *second* point, centering yourself in your actuality, like accepting things out of your control, allows you to be humble, thankful, and see things as they are. Then, you will not be swept away by a misguided sense of justice or privilege. Gratitude helps release us from the entitlement that many struggle with. Now, you might see that word entitlement and bristle. You might think you're not very entitled at all. This is possible, but I suspect for many of us, at least in the United States (as well as much of the Western world), we struggle with expecting more than we have, while already having more than those around us.

By centering yourself in actuality, you have knowledge of the way things are, not just the way things should be. Let's look at the latter in order to understand the former. When we expect things to be a certain way, we are drawing on a sense of justice in the world. This can be a good thing. If we expect that our work is rewarded and good wins out over evil, justice is served. When we believe in meritocracy, where the most qualified, best individuals are given what they have "earned," we are setting a standard that should be applied universally. Many would see this as a good thing. We are setting a balanced, fair standard for life where those who cheat, who lie, and who steal are punished for their crimes, even in small things.

On the other hand, a sense of entitlement, of expectations based on what we perceive we are owed, can go horribly wrong. If you haven't been told yet: life isn't fair. This is one of the biggest struggles I have experienced in my own life. You will not get the job you deserve based wholly on merit. You will most likely not get the recognition you "deserve." You might, but you aren't owed it, nor should you expect it. We'll talk more about expectations with our third major point in a minute, but what you expect is not always (or often) the reality. You might have to do four times the work to get the same recognition as someone else. You might have to toil for years. This doesn't mean you should stop pushing; it means you should never give up. The work you choose to do in life, whether it be spiritual or temporal, or (hopefully) both, should be done because it is worth doing. Does this mean you should skip menial tasks because they are not worthwhile? No. Again, no. These tasks, despite having value in themselves, are connected to your larger goals and fulfillment. If you work a menial job in order to pay bills and feed yourself, is this not worthwhile? The key is not to see your identity in your work, or at least fully in your work. We may all have a variety of jobs in our lives, but we are still who we are. The underlying character is what keeps us grounded and creates an unstoppable force. If you let others, or even ourselves, define us by our work, our looks, our financial standing, etc., we are giving up our character, our very selves, to the power of others. Ultimately, I believe our identity should be in our faith and in our God, but again, even if we reject this foundation, we still make choices about our identity every day that affect our agency.

How does this connect back to gratitude? This is related to the earlier-mentioned issue of false ambitions. Are our ambitions caused by a need to please others who may or may not matter? Or ourselves? Or our God? Or others who do matter? I might take a detour by suggesting that working to please others can be valuable, but it must be the right "others." Do you work because your family requires your work to sustain them? That is valuable. Do you help others so they might be bettered? That is valuable. But the underlying motivation should not be because you want kudos or recognition, because, first, this is out of your control, and second, it is hollow. You should help others because your character demands it. Gratitude (following from humility) helps us to control these impulses by re-centering us in our obligations to God and ourselves. Seeing things as they actually are in reality is an essential part of this. Why? Because then we do not have delusions about what should or should not be. God will take care of what is just. We should strive for justice in our lives by *doing* what is just. Justice goes wrong when it becomes an imposition on other competing forms of "justice," rooted in misguided philosophy. This is why one's faith is an essential part of seeing things as they are. If you believe in ultimate justice through God, then you are freed from the need to fix everything to make it fair. Again, this life is not fair. This becomes an impossible expectation and leads us astray from the realities we *can* control to better ourselves and those around us. Which leads us to maxim number three.

Third, when faced with a new reality, expectations change, including relationship expectations. An event such as a pandemic re-centers our thinking. It strips away the mirage of fairness, or expectations, of a sanitized, safe life. When you first heard you would be staying home for work during this past pandemic, how many of you were happy? How many were happy after a week or two? I'm guessing a number of you in this boat ended up very happy. The expectations of putting on airs for coworkers and bosses were gone. Clients and customers might have expected less. The expectations were significantly lowered. Now, this assumes you had a job where you could stay home and still make a living. Many of you were not in this situation. Many of you persevered and worked harder and longer to keep the economy running. Many of you lost your jobs; though you may have had fewer manufactured expectations, you also had the immense stress of trying to make a living. For a minute, let's set that aside, difficult as that may be, to focus on what removed expectations looks like. For those of you who continued to go to work, you didn't meet lowered expectations because your job didn't have some of those expectations in the first place. But for those who had the luxury of working from home, I'm guessing many of you found that the time you spent on wasteful encounters, relationships, and "work" was severely limited. There is loneliness, there are other difficulties, but the kind of false expectations we feel in life were gone. No need to stress about what someone thinks of you, or if you did the right thing at work when those situations are removed.

You might also have found that the people who did bother to keep in touch and spend time with you were your true friends. When someone doesn't have to connect with you, or more likely doesn't feel like they have to, they won't. It's the old adage of true friends being the ones who are there for you when times are difficult. In the pandemic, relationships started to self-select even further, because connection was more difficult to have. It was easier to just avoid people or situations that cause undue stress. This is a quite complex network of both relationship and expectation that each of us find ourselves caught in, in very different ways. Suffice it to say, the concept that has come out of all this, at least for me, is that of expectations. Difficult situations give us a reset that provides us respite from the anxiety and busyness that we face in everyday life. We now have time to step outside of this web of interaction and see where the unnecessary connections lie. The many memes aimed at introverts about needing to recharge or being happy to avoid social situations are exacerbated by the continuous stream of frivolous interactions we have in life, both virtually and in person. And I say this as one who is not overly introverted. I like to see people. However, our attention is continually in demand from sources that have no right to expect it. To use the current example, the pandemic has silenced many of those voices. It has forced us to interact with our children, spouses, and those who need and deserve it the most. It has lifted the veil of false expectations at work, giving us a needed perspective on what is truly important in our lives. The trick moving forward is to take this insight and apply it to future life. We must abandon these false relationships, these false goals, and focus on what is truly valuable. Difficulty can refocus our time where it belongs. That is why, hard as it might be, it is important to look at times of stress as a blessing with which to re-center our priorities.

Further, being distant from others creates a longing for true relationship, for true value in our work. Knowing now how precious our time is, and how limited it is (in addition to the reminder of life's frailty), we are propelled to be wise in our lives. For many, this time has been a chance to think and write and meditate on what will be. It was a forced break from the monotony of busyness that leads to anxiety—anxiety swelling forth from our continual work and the occupation of our time. We don't spend time with those that matter, even when we do. We don't work toward the goals we have, the things we truly value. We work for the appearance of respect and respectfulness. Extreme difficulty frees us to reset our values—to allow the virtue that we know is at our core to surface. Perhaps this is not what you feel. Perhaps you feel adrift in a sea of loneliness and anxiety. This is a chance to abandon the foundation of sand you have built on, the one built on the expectations and vices of others. It is a chance to build (or rebuild) your character. The character you know you should have but have never pursued. The foundation of rock that will not be swayed. Your darkest hour is a chance for you to come out stronger. To have purpose. To have peace.

By resetting and meditating/accepting these three things, we bring in a *time of healing*. The body needs rest, as does the soul, and in our current world this becomes very hard. Our society is built on hurry, which leads to anxiety. In a constant state of anxiety, we cannot function properly. We cannot be what our Creator intended us to be. Although it is paradoxical, a time of intense anxiety can lead us to peace. The fire that threatens our existence, hardens our resolve. By accepting these three maxims, we are freed to refocus on our purpose, on our being as humans created in the image of God. The very thing that threatens our existence heals our souls from the damage that life has inflicted upon us.

In the following pages, I will lead us through the virtues that are at the core of our existence, that guide us to peace in all contexts. This time is an opportunity to release our soul to freedom.

First, we will look at some background on virtue, and then meditate on the key virtues I've chosen. Think through them. Use them as you will. They are tested over the course of thousands of years. Perhaps nothing truly new is contained here, but we all need to be refreshed and reawakened to the core of our character at times. I hope this text does that for you. One of the main reasons a refocusing on virtue is so revitalizing is because it connects to something we already know to be true. You may not be learning anything, but you are releasing the power of truth. As you read, realize that truth undergirds all of these virtues. Authenticity of self is something that must never be downplayed.

Personally, I believe true freedom comes in the knowledge of Jesus Christ, and that virtue springs forth from the Trinitarian God of the Scriptures. Jesus said, "'I am the way, and the truth, and the life. No one comes to the Father except through me.'"[1] You'll see that faith in Christ woven into this book and the account of my thoughts. But as I've alluded to already, whether you have or will accept Jesus as the Christ, you may resonate with what I'm sharing here on life and virtue. I'm not sharing this just to write a book. I know that these pages contain a series of ruminations that you may or may not connect to. You may not appreciate the way I've organized my thoughts. You may outright be hostile to them. This isn't meant to appease you. It is just a record of these thoughts for myself, my family, and anyone else who might be interested. Take it with a grain of salt, or take it as the opening to a conversation. But I know that the virtues and the realizations I've come to, that are crystalized in these pages, are useful to me, and I hope they are useful to you. If one concept triggers a series of changes or foci in your life that lead to peace, that lead to success, then it will have been a worthwhile read.

---

1. John 14:6, NRSV.

2

The Foundations of Virtue

Virtue, then, is of two kinds: that of the intellect and that of character.
Intellectual virtue owes its origin and development mainly to teaching,
for which reason its attainment requires experience and time; virtue of
character (*ēthos*) is a result of habituation (*ethos*), for which reason it
has acquired its name through a small variation on '*ethos*'.[1]

I N THIS QUOTE FROM Aristotle's *Nicomachean Ethics* we see
the basis for the development of virtue in early Christianity,
where our discussion begins. If we take Aristotle's view of virtue
being formed by habit, then this creates a path for us to build our
character through daily living and good habits. Virtue, then, is
not something that we either have or don't have. It is something
that has been cultivated, built, and resides within us due to a long-
term practice of virtue building. That said, I do believe there is
more to character than just this. For one, you must have the desire
to cultivate virtues, as well as the habits in place with which to
build that character. One of the biggest mistakes that we make,

1. Aristotle, *Nicomachean Ethics*, Book II, Chapter 1, 23.

both individually and as a society, is assigning talent, abilities, or character to someone as an inherent trait. Let me expand on this.

This takes place most clearly when we look at someone with a particular talent such as an artist or a baseball player, both skills that take physical effort. Many will say, "I cannot do that," but what they are really saying is that either they do not know, or do not have the desire to do that. Clearly, some people have more ability than others when it comes to painting a painting or hitting a breaking ball, but it is something that one can get better at should they have the desire. Character can be viewed in the same way through the virtues. Habits can be built to strengthen one's virtue. As after years of training even a modest artist might become quite good with longstanding habits, a person struggling with vices may strengthen their character to live life to its fullest after an extended period of practice. This is borne out specifically in the Christian tradition, which is the place from which I write. Again, I think that you can cultivate virtue outside of this tradition, but I believe it is best cultivated within it. If you do not agree, please take my work here as a starting point that you can appropriate to your own situation. Take this as my experience, my testimonial based on many failures leading to some rudimentary level of enlightenment, or at least enlightenment in progress—because character comes through habit, and is not something held on to without continued work.

In the fourth century, Christianity faced a pivotal point in its history. The third century had been filled with Roman persecution and the church, though established, was forced to deal with the continuing reality of martyrdom and suffering that had continued since the time of Christ. Martyrdom is a display of the ultimate in commitment, in one's character—to be willing to die for something they believe in. It's hard to fake martyrdom. If given the opportunity to recant a belief, one who is not committed would likely choose to live and turn back on their own beliefs. Even those who truly believe may fear death more than their belief allows. The martyr chooses to die as a witness to the truth of their belief. Could this be a false belief? Certainly. But there is a clear commitment to their own faith. In fact, in early Christianity there was an issue with the craving of martyrdom, perhaps beyond what is now considered healthy. Read Ignatius of Antioch's "Letter to the Romans" and you'll find a quite aggressive and eager approach to his own death. We see martyrdom starting in the first century with Stephen in the book of Acts, then Polycarp, to Cyprian of Carthage in 258 AD, to name some notable martyrs.

However, this is a digression. We start our story in the fourth century, in 313, with the Edict of Milan. The Emperor Constantine supposedly saw a sign of the cross in the sky, and was told, "In this sign, conquer." From that moment on, for better or worse, Christianity was linked with the secular world and the concept of empire. The reason that I mentioned the previous martyrs is because for about 300 years, Christianity was an "outsider" religion. It was persecuted and stood in opposition to the Roman Empire, in one way or another. With Constantine's revelation, things were about to change rapidly. The Edict of Milan made it legal for Christianity to be practiced. Contrary to popular belief, it did not make Christianity the official religion of the empire, though soon this would be the default. Shortly after this edict, in 325, the Council of Nicaea was held. This was the place where Christians would hammer out the Nicene Creed, which began the work of crystalizing the doctrine of the Trinity—later finalized in 381 at the Council of Constantinople. It is these years that are crucial to our study.

With the move to put Christianity in the mainstream, many Christians began to see a divide in how faith was practiced. It was this divide that led some to the Egyptian desert, where asceticism was practiced by the Desert Fathers. These fathers are known for their wisdom sayings, but their monastic practices in the desert paralleled what we see in the Greek philosophers. Philosophy in Ancient Greece was not just a way of thinking, but was also a way of life. It was a lifestyle that followers immersed themselves in.[2] In the desert, Christians could avoid the secularized version of Christianity that was forming in the empire, and seek out a Christianity that was perceived as "purer," removed from the developments in Rome. This form of Christianity was built on monastic habit

---

2. See Hadot, *Philosophy as a Way of Life*, 82–83.

and character formation. It was a form of purification, aspiring to cleanse the soul of impurity. We see a major example of this in the person of Evagrius Ponticus.

Now, if you'll allow me to digress for a moment (and since I'm the author, you don't really have a choice), I do want to emphasize that I do not necessarily think that the desert Christians have a purer form of Christianity or virtue than those in the urban regions of the time. They do, however, present us with a method of virtue formation that is valuable to all. One of the errors many people make is to look at those who have removed themselves from the world as more pious, or more holy. Though there is much to be admired about this kind of separation, it is more difficult to live a life of good character and virtue within the centers of culture and commerce. Constant temptation and distraction awaits us. Again, this is one of the benefits of a pandemic or other major life event—it gives us a chance to step outside this distraction and focus on what is important to us, both personally and as a community. On the other hand, being alone with one's thoughts can also be a significant challenge, and one of the reasons that character formation through virtue is so important.

As we look back to the desert, we see the figure of Evagrius Ponticus. The average person, or even Christian, probably doesn't know who he is. This is partly due to the fact that his writings were deemed heretical many years after his death (in 553 AD), and partly due to the fact that his work on the "eight thoughts" was supplanted by a more popular version in the Western church—the seven deadly sins. Evagrius was born in 345 in what is now Asia Minor. After a very promising theological career with the Cappadocian Fathers[3] was derailed by impropriety, he ended up in the Egyptian desert for the last portion of his life. Like many of us who have made errors in our lives, the desert offered him a chance at redemption by developing what is now one of the great theological systems of prayer in the Christian tradition.

---

3. The Cappadocian Fathers—Gregory Nazianzen, Gregory of Nyssa, and Basil the Great—all were key players in the fourth century Trinitarian and christological discussions, hammering out Christian doctrine on key issues.

For purposes of our book, I want to focus on the eight thoughts. They played into a larger system of prayer that was aimed at overcoming demons and connecting to God Himself. You probably know the seven deadly sins: gluttony, lust, anger, greed, sloth, envy, and pride. Using that as a starting point, Evagrius' thoughts might look familiar: gluttony, fornication, anger, avarice, acedia, sadness, vainglory, and pride. The differences are subtle, but important. The first four match up directly with the seven deadly sins, but the last four are variations. Acedia is like sloth, but is centered around distraction versus laziness. Sadness is a kind of envy, but an envy of one's previous life. Remember, these teachings were aimed at monks, so looking back on the life they had left behind would be a significant temptation. Lastly, pride in Gregory's seven deadly sins is divided into two categories in Evagrius' eight: vainglory, which is pride directed at other humans, and pride, which is pride against God, a much more serious offense.[4] Remember that Evagrius preceded Gregory and was really the fountainhead for the seven deadly sins. So, the next time you hear them mentioned, know that an earlier monk was actually the originator of this system of vices.

But knowing about vices doesn't do a lot of good without understanding a way to combat them. Evagrius does this also, using a system of prayer. Specifically, he has a treatise entitled *On the Vices Opposed to the Virtues* that connected these eight thoughts, as well as jealousy to make nine, with a list of virtues. They connect as follows: gluttony–abstinence, fornication–chastity, avarice–freedom from possessions, sadness–joy, anger–patience, acedia–perseverance, vainglory–freedom from vainglory, jealousy–freedom from jealousy, and lastly, pride–humility.[5] In these pairings, we can see that some of the virtues I mentioned earlier are present, or at least adjacently present. We'll get to that a bit later. What we do see in Evagrius' system is a series of foundational thoughts that tempt

4. See Tsakiridis, *Evagrius Ponticus*, for more information on Evagrius and the eight thoughts.

5. Evagrius, "On the Vices Opposed to the Virtues," 1–9, in *Evagrius of Pontus*, 62–65.

us to sin and keep us from the person of God. He goes into great detail in explaining how these thoughts work and what they do to us. He presents a system to combat them that is based in prayer and habit, and also shows some psychological depth, especially considering we are talking about writings over 1,600 years old. Foundationally, Evagrius gives us a path to becoming close to God. Starting with meditation/prayer on the material world, he moves toward the immaterial world, and ultimately to the place of God. The process starts where the monk starts. One is not expected to see the face of God without a long path of prayer and meditation. This presumably would take years. In the same way that Aristotle speaks of habit, and Evagrius gives us a model of how to use it, we must build habits that focus on key virtues in order to escape the prison of vice in which we find ourselves trapped in the modern world. Just as the Christians of the fourth century fled to the desert to escape the world, we too must escape to build our character and our virtue.[6]

So, am I suggesting that we run off to the desert for a while? While not a bad idea—we all need to reset and recharge—what I am suggesting is that times of difficulty might be used to reset our character. It is a time to build habits that can be used to strengthen ourselves in this world. Sometimes we are given the gift of a forced "desert." Instead of complaining and moaning about it, we might use it to fortify ourselves for the upcoming battles we face in life—and we will face them. Times of difficulty are actually an opening to catch up on our character formation. It's an opportunity disguised as a trial. It is my hope that moving forward in life you, and I, can see trials as opportunities to build our character, and reminders that we need to keep ourselves strong. This will also prepare us so that the next trial will be less difficult. Despite the many warnings we've heard in fables, parables, children's stories, and even adult education, we tend to procrastinate. We put things off. We try to get by.

6. For more on habit in early Christianity see Tsakiridis, "Habit as a Spiritual Discipline," 77–88.

Don't try to get by. Build yourself up so that you are not just passing the bar, but are so far above it that the bar is no longer a thought. Strong character allows us to walk through life as *our true selves*. We will not be brought down by the demons in life if we approach each encounter as a great challenge. See the challenge within yourself. Build your spiritual life. Then those challenges will have already been won in your training. Often it is a huge psychological difficulty to deal with changes in life; building virtue allows you to take these changes in stride, knowing who you are and that you will handle them.

I know some of you may find yourself flatfooted against the changing trials of the modern world. Social media has us in a state of constant anxiety. Teleconferences and emails have become worse since 2020, and will probably continue to be that way. Anxiety is no longer just something that we face in encounters in locations outside our home; they now are a part of our inner life. We cannot escape these stresses without being deliberate about it. Although I think it is important to isolate these factors and reduce them, once your inner-self is strengthened, these stressors become less important, and less tempting.

That said, let's get back to these early Christians. In the desert these believers struggled with demons and difficulties that forged their virtuous character. If you read the Desert Fathers you will find allusions to the cardinal virtues discussed in this book. They talk about habits and virtues in a setting of spiritual warfare, while struggling inwardly with vices. Whether their stories are metaphorical or literal, they paint the picture of wisdom combatting temptation. When it comes down to it, there is a core way to fight evil in the life of the Christian—by reading the Bible and praying. For many of you this may sound familiar. Though it isn't presented in the ubiquitous way it was when we were kids, the old directive to read your Bible daily and pray to God regularly is actually great advice for the Christian. If you are not a follower of Christ, you might expand this basic concept to say you should read wisdom literature and meditate every day, but the idea that we should be focused on our core beliefs is an essential one for building our character.[7] And by focusing on those core beliefs we will reinforce them, whether they be good or not. So, choose wisely. The habit of reading Scripture and praying is the engine through which we begin to build that character. I find it a bit funny because this was the message drilled into me as a child in an evangelical church . . . and school . . . and everywhere. I found it kind of boring. I felt like this is something I should do, but it wasn't fun. It wasn't relevant enough. Part of this reaction is being a kid, so if you're like me, do forgive yourself for not paying attention sooner. But that simple message connects to a rich history of biblical and patristic (relating to the Church Fathers) wisdom. Just like the simplicity of the Christian Gospel has immense depth, the simplicity of this message is a key to building habit and virtue in life. Ultimately this leads to a more fulfilling, more peaceful existence. This basic message leads us to an understanding that unlocks a host of virtue. Just like when someone tells us to exercise to get in shape, we often ignore them. Is exercise an easy concept to understand? Of course. Is it easy to execute? Not always. It's the same in building virtue through habit. Start where you are and do it. Keep doing it. It gets easier. Better to do a little prayer and meditation every day than none. You build strength by building upon strength.

One of the biggest lies of the modern age is that people either have an ability or they don't. That it's just about genetics or talent or socialization. It isn't. Those things help (sometimes a lot), but if you just start doing something and keep doing it you will enhance your skill at it. It may take a little while or (more likely) a long while, but you will get better. Building strong habits allows you to build virtue, character, or whatever you are trying to build. By the same token, if you continue to commit to a habit rooted in vice, you will continue that activity. The longer it goes on, the harder it will be to break. I'm guessing you already know this. Start now and build habits of virtue, and those habits will sustain you in life. You can't build up

7. Again, I believe, as a Christian, that the best way to find peace is through Jesus Christ and that reading the Bible and praying to the Trinitarian God is the best avenue. I do also believe, however, that there can be value in meditation and reading wisdom from other sources. Though not the ideal, it is still quite useful.

muscle then stop exercising and expect the muscle to stay. Virtue is the same. You can't stop practicing the core habits that build up your virtue lest you fall back into the old vices of life. Start now.

3

Humility

N OW THAT THE FOUNDATIONS have been laid, let us think about the seven virtues alluded to in the title of this book. Each of these has been chosen deliberately to fit into a system of virtue practice, building on the "pre-virtue" of honesty, which is the foundation of many virtues. We begin with a basic virtue in religious tradition: humility.

When we think of the virtue of humility we typically think of lowering ourselves beneath others. Some think of it as showing deference. Some think of it as not being boastful. Although it can be all these things, they tend to miss the point. I define humility as seeing yourself as you truly are. And if you've seen a pattern in this book, one of the major themes is seeing things (and yourself) as they truly are. Let's use that as our starting point for a definition—*humility is seeing yourself as you truly are.*[1]

I think I could almost stop and let us meditate on that for a while. In fact, if you have the time, try to do just that. Take a few minutes (or more) and think about what this really means. Focus on the word *humility*.

---

1. For a helpful discussion on humility, see Bondi, *To Love as God Loves*, 41–56, specifically the ancient view on pages 42–43.

Now that you've done that, let's break down what this is actually all about. In religious texts, as well as society, we see the term humility all over the place, especially when talking about Christianity and Christian virtue. If pride is the ultimate sin, and following both the biblical text and Evagrius' desert teachings I think you can make that case, then we must remedy that somehow. Humility is the answer. If humility is seeing oneself as they are in actuality, it does a few things. First, it roots us in truth and honesty, which, as I stated earlier, is the foundational virtue for many, if not all, of the virtues we are discussing in this book. Humility often brings us down to earth because we already have an inflated view of ourselves. We have an overestimated view of what we are owed—what we deserve. Humility strips away the concept of what is deserved, especially in the light of Christian belief. If you believe that you are sinful—and I think most would agree on this point, whether they use that language or not—then you deserve far worse than what you have been given. Humility allows us to see our shortcomings in the light of truth. There is nowhere to hide when this light is shone.

Let's think of this in the light of our relationship with God. We will always fall short of God. We are limited, finite, flawed. This is not to say that we don't have many perceived good qualities, but in the light of God, we are nothing. This is a comparison we should always have, always see, because it keeps us rooted in humility. Perhaps, you don't like this parallel, and you want to take this comparison to the secular world and measure yourself against others. In this endeavor you will also find that you often fall short. You can always find something that you are better at than someone else; you can find their flaws and know that often they are not your own. This, however, is just a temporary salve on the wound of insecurity. It makes you feel better temporarily, but does not treat the actual wound of our pride. Pride often arises from insecurity as a response to overestimate our abilities or deserts. Be humble and focus on your own spiritual life, your own character. Know that you are always short of perfection, and ignoring these comparisons with other people will lead to lasting peace.

This explains why people hate humility so much. It is why many turn to a false humility, trying to strike a balance by not looking proud, yet not allowing the truth of humility to show our actual selves. For most of us, this would feel like the ultimate disaster. What happens in times of crisis is that the structures and façades that cover our weaknesses—the ones we hide behind—are no longer there. This may allow us to hide from others, because we can hole up while working from home or avoiding social situations, but it does not allow us to hide from ourselves. If your identity has been formed by your job or your friends or your accomplishments, they are shown to be less valuable than you thought they were when they all go away or are forgotten. Even from a purely economic standpoint, you see whose work is important and whose is less so in light of economic crisis. And what we find is that the "good" jobs that are respectable to upper-middle class Americans are not as important to the survival of humanity as we might think they are. This is not to say that your work or my work is not valuable. However, what it should do is let you know that the person you look down upon is the person whose shoulders you sometimes stand on. Perhaps their character is stronger than you realize. Again, this is not to attack vocations or employment. It is, however, to show truth and humble us to the reality of our existence.

This ties in to another reason we fear humility—perceived respect. Look at any series of self-help or entrepreneurial motivations and you will continually see the theme of respect. Personally, this is one of the toughest for me. Even in writing this, there is an authenticity that must be shown in that I struggle with respect. However, the fact of the matter is that the struggle for respect with others is really a struggle with respect for ourselves. We don't feel that others respect us because, perhaps, we are not happy with what we are doing. We aren't doing the things we should. Our character is shown to be flawed against the standard that *we have set*. This is good news! Although it may not seem like it, it is valuable to be able to admit this. Through the admission of our own shortcomings we accept humility. We accept things as they truly are. And what they are is not what you want them to be. These are not false expectations, these are factual realities. The fact that you don't respect yourself because you are falling short of your own acceptable character levels is also a good sign. This means that internally you know what standard you should be at, and are falling short of that standard. You can't run a race if you don't know where the finish line is. If you know what your character should look like, this is the first step in beginning habits to form that character. You already know who you are in your essence. You must now conform reality to that internal knowledge. Humility allows us to see ourselves as we are, so that we can become who we are meant to be.

Further, because our humility is ignored, we try to be respectable in an attempt to obtain admiration. You will not earn respect by feigning to be respectable. You must actually form your character, make strong choices and do what is necessary. Hence, respect is not something you look for in worldly institutions or other people. It comes as a result of humility and doing your work, both in the mundane and the spiritual. In other words, do your work well both in your career and at home, and build your spiritual life through prayer, meditation, and reading the Bible (or the wisdom literature you use—see my earlier note on this) and this will lead to the change you seek. As it says in the book of Colossians, "Whatever your task, put yourselves into it, as done for the Lord and not for your masters."[2]

This morning I walked to work. The leaves are changing in the residential neighborhood I live in. The air is a crisp fall air. It was perfect for clearing my head and focusing on my tasks this morning, such as writing this reflection. It reminded me that the simple things we can do are actually more important to our well-being than the difficult things. Something as simple as going for a walk is a great way to clear one's head. Ideally, we do this in nature, but some of us must use the nature in our communities. The setting will look different for everyone. I love to walk in large cities surrounded by tall buildings, trains, and other infrastructure.[3]

2. Col 3:23, NRSV.

3. I would wager this is in large part because I grew up in the city of Chicago with an "el" train running over my street. The nostalgia of home is often a

This has its own peace for me. Find what works for you. Part of doing the previously mentioned work is engaging in simple things that re-center our inner consciousness.

In this vein, we often try to be seen by others in our activities. We don't do things because they form our character, but because we get accolades for them. This undermines the whole process of humility and character formation. In an attempt to get something the cheap way, we miss out on the foundation, the roots of what will bring us the long-term satisfaction we crave. This is true in both a spiritual sense and a secular one. Be humble. Do the hard work of character formation. I don't think I truly understood the story of the tortoise and the hare until I was well into my adulthood. The idea that "slow and steady wins the race" is foreign to us, no matter how much we know its truth. We want things now. When we look for that quick fix of "respect" by being seen doing things, we miss out on the steady progress that will lead to actual respect for our accomplishments. In other words, by not worrying about the reward, it may come to you in a better way than you anticipated. Just like the constant theme in Scripture, your intentions and internal direction are what is most important. What comes out—the results—are just the outpouring of that. Again, this is true in both spiritual formation and the mundane work of life. As Jesus states in the Gospel of Mark, "There is nothing outside a person that by going in can defile, but the things that come out are what defile."[4] Our character and inner spiritual life determine what comes out of us. Let's stop blaming outside factors for our own actions. Let humility abound and let us see ourselves as we are.

In the past couple of years, I came to a realization about respect. We must understand intentions when dealing with disrespect and slights. If someone does something to upset you, think about the two major motivations that might cause this. One, they might have made a mistake, and it was unintentional. If this is the case, you should let it go and forgive because there was no malice.

---

place to settle our spirit. This may not always be the case, but I believe it holds true for many of us.

4. Mark 7:15, NRSV

Two, if they intentionally did it to slight you, their intention is to provoke a reaction, or hurt, in which case you should also ignore it because by getting angry you are giving them exactly what they want. In either case, you should let go of small slights and markers of disrespect. If you are confident in your humility and know who you are, these small things should pass over you without attachment. Now, I'm not saying I've mastered this. I believe very strongly in people having respect for each other, but respecting yourself and your relationship with God frees you to dismiss the kind of inconsequential disrespect that you encounter in everyday life. This is done both through humility and forgiveness.

Again, through this line of thinking, we see that humility allows us to conquer our fear of perceived slight. Respect comes through virtue—humility, diligence, and love. By now you might start to see a pattern. Humility is not weakness, or lowering yourself. It's being confident in who you are, not faking bravado, but actual confidence that allows you to admit your shortcomings. At the very least this should be admitted to yourself, but beyond this, it is at times helpful to admit weakness in public. By admitting this weakness, you are, at least in the right circumstances, showing strength. It is the strength that says, "No matter how you react to this, I will handle it." Whether that be through words or physical defense, you will handle the situation that comes. I know this sounds odd, but usually with this confidence comes a welcome reception to connect, to bond with another person. As a side tip, this is a great approach to public speaking: when you go in front of people fully confident in who *you* are, you are freed to be yourself and say what you need to say. You are not afraid of people seeing the real you because you are expecting them to see the real you and all that this entails. This same truth comes through in everyday life. Humility is freedom. It is being yourself, doing what you need to do, and not worrying about what others think. This is to be clearly distinguished from selfishness. When I say "not worrying about what others think" it is because you are confident in your own character and virtue. You know who you are in relation to God and others and have nothing to worry about. It is not being a jerk and letting others deal with the fallout of your anger. The person formed in character can be confident in this way because they care for others, because they do what is right in the sight of God and humanity. This is a key point. Where much self-help goes wrong is that it tells you to do what you want, and damn anyone who disagrees. That is *not* what I am saying. What I am proposing is that if you already are rooted in your character with humility, what you want will be good, because you are acting out of truth, acting out of love toward God, yourself, and others.

Therefore, humility is freedom in truth. It is knowing yourself in the light of truth. Truth and honesty are always the foundation. How do you practically access humility? Well, first of all you spend time in prayer and Scripture. Meditating on good things and being honest with yourself in the light of God is where the foundation starts. This leads to a better sense of self, and with a better sense of self, you see yourself honestly and in an authentic way. Second, you can start to implement this in your everyday life—being observant of how you behave in relationship with others, or even when you are alone. Then you will start to see how your actions spring forth from your attitude. Mindfulness of yourself and your relationships is key in understanding humility, and many of the virtues we will discuss. That's another reason why, as I've alluded to a number of times, even if you are not coming from faith in Christ, these principles will still apply. We see this in Buddhism and other religious traditions. I think there are many reasons to be a Christian, and I believe virtue springs from He who is virtuous—the Trinitarian God, but that doesn't mean that elements of the truth of that virtue are not available to all who seek it. However, I do believe without the foundation of belief in the One who is virtuous, it is just a shadow of what it can be. I will try to avoid making this distinction in future chapters, but know, again, that even if you are not a follower of Christianity, virtuous behavior is something we all should attempt to attain in our lives.

To sum up, humility is something we all should strive for, and is accessible. If we can be humble, building on the truth we find at our core character, we are on the path to all of these other virtues.

Humility builds on truth. You can start with any of the virtues, as long as honesty is the core character trait, but starting with humility makes many of the other virtues easier to access. Humility is strength. Don't let anyone tell you otherwise. You can do great things if you know who you are in the light of God.

4

Gratitude

F LOWING OUT OF HUMILITY is gratitude. As I've previously
mentioned, gratitude is one of the things that was really reinforced for me this past year. It isn't that I did not already know
I should be grateful. In fact, over the past several years, as I struggled with a less-than-satisfying career, and originally conceived of
a book dealing with virtue, it was one of the three I started with:
humility, gratitude, and diligence. It's just that when a pandemic
hit and I started to see the lack of control I actually had, it pointed
me back to gratitude. When you see people lose their jobs around
you, yet yours remains, it creates gratitude. When you see people
dying of something uncontrollable, you become grateful. Remember, when the pandemic first started really hitting the United States
in March of 2020, there was a lot of uncertainty and a lot of fear. I
saw the local grocery store look closer to a Soviet era market than
any time in my lifetime. That said, the supply lines still held up
incredibly well and the store was full of food. In fact, to bring it
back, over the next several months, the distribution lines held up
very well: another reason to be grateful; back then fear of the worst
was on the horizon.

Furthermore, there wasn't a lot we could do about this fear. People were hoarding food, and closing themselves off in their homes. Online retailers were getting hit hard also. Preppers across the country must have rejoiced as their day had come. To watch your expected supply lines disappear, if only temporarily, creates a lot of fear. Besides the obvious lesson that perhaps we should have more supplies in our homes than most people typically do, it also is a reminder that even in the United States, the breadbasket of the world, a food shortage could happen more quickly than you think. There are a number of biblical lessons that come to mind here, both in being wise in the ways of the world and being grateful and dependent upon God for what we do have. Gratitude flows out of the notion that you do not deserve what you have—that you are blessed to have food, water, shelter. We take these basic things for granted, and even when continually reminded that we shouldn't, we still do. Feeling fear, feeling hungry, feeling thirsty reminds us to be grateful for what we do have. That is why the person who seemingly struggles is the one who often seems grateful, and the one who has abundance never seems to have enough.

Gratitude is also a result of humility. As stated previously, humility allows us to see things as they are, and this in turn, allows us to see how we are blessed by the things we do have. My approach from a perspective of virtue is to do the things that we "should" be doing. We should be honest. We should be humble. We should be grateful. We should be diligent. We should build our character, starting with the virtues in this book. If we do those things, the things we want will come to us. And the less we want them, and the more we focus on our character, the more they may come—or at least it might seem like it. Because we won't care. Our focus will be on something that we can control—ourselves. It's a lot easier to avoid frustration if you avoid putting your satisfaction in the hands of others. By being grateful, you deflect expectation and entitlement. When accomplishments come, they are a byproduct of what we are doing; they are not an expectation that what we do requires that byproduct. To simplify, focus on what you can control, and the rest will come to you. This is not to say that we shouldn't set goals and accomplish them, but set goals that you can accomplish. Do not set goals that require someone else's approval or judgment. That gets tricky, because much is out of our control. So, control what you can and let things come as they come. I know there are some theological sticky points here. Some might say that we cannot control ourselves, and such is the nature of sin. Some will disagree. Either way, for the Christian, you can control yourself through the power of the Holy Spirit. We all fail along our path, but the true failure is to stop and give in to what is preventing you from your goal of good character.

But let's get back to gratitude. Why is gratitude such an important virtue? After humility, *it is the foundation of letting go of expectation and entitlement.* These virtues build a two-pronged attack on our pride and feelings of desert—feeling we are owed something. How do you foster gratitude? The same way we foster humility—by setting aside the current circumstances we have created in our lives and by seeing things as they really are. When we look to ourselves and start to list the things we should be grateful for, it tends to start the inertia of gratitude. Do you have any clothing? Be grateful. Did you eat today? Be grateful. What tends to happen is that we see those things as entitlements. Everyone gets clothing, everyone eats, so I deserve more. No, they don't and no you don't. We have been so successful in the West that for the most part, even our poor are doing well. Some perspective on how good you have it might help you. The funny thing is, the person reading this book who might actually need more clothing or food might be the person more likely to take the advice to heart. Why? Because they know they are not in control. They haven't built up a false façade of humility and entitlement. That isn't to say that pride and selfishness don't come to everyone; they do in one way or another. However, knowing you can't always control where your next meal is coming from helps you let go of those expectations. As I've alluded to already, and will do more of as this book moves forward, this must be balanced with diligence and agency. In other words, we need to be grateful for what we have, yet continually strive to move forward—to work and build so that we have control over the things we can control. But make no mistake, there are things out of your control. They might wipe you out; they might take away all you've earned. And in that time, you must surrender to God in humility. So why not take the path of gratitude in the first place? Why not enjoy life?

So, let's try to be practical. How can we increase our gratitude? First, we must set aside our expectations. Step outside of yourself and look at things objectively. Basically, you want to wipe away the network of structures you have in your life that create expectations. Go back to the core of what is important to you—your values, character, and goals. Do this as a mental exercise. Find out what is really important to you. This doesn't mean you should abrogate your commitments like marriage, family, contracts, etc. Your character should not allow that. Your character is still foundational to this exercise. What I'm saying is to strip away all that extra stuff and get to the core of your character and faith. Second, spend time in quiet with this. Read Scripture, wisdom literature, and pray. Fill your mind with good things, and quiet yourself. We might liken some of this to the Buddhist ideal of mindfulness. Be hyper-aware of your station in life and your surroundings. This might take a long time, or it might already be percolating within you, and you are letting it out . . . finally. You're being honest with yourself. That's also why humility is a precursor to gratitude. The honesty in humility allows you to be grateful.

Once you've reached this stage, start making a practice of being grateful, either in your prayers or by making a list. Let it be a reflex. When you start to feel down, list three things you are grateful for, and meditate on that. Don't just go through the motions. One of the biggest problems people have in acquiring skills or habits is that they think that if they just put in the time, they will master something. But if you don't have intention, you are wasting a good deal of energy. This is the problem with our school system. It encourages finishing each year and getting good grades, but not actual learning or mastery. Learning does come with this process, but it is not the ultimate goal for students. It's almost more of a byproduct. I think people approach their inner life the same way at times. They do it half-heartedly and then wonder why nothing changes.

On the other hand, if you are having trouble getting your mind to set aside the grid of distraction in your life, you can flip this process and start by being grateful and then work toward understanding your situation. But no matter where you start, the key is intention. You must have intention in your actions. Again, this connects to the concept of diligence and agency. Gratitude arises from humility, which then points us to diligence and agency. Once we understand our true circumstances, and are grateful for where we are, we are ready to move forward. I've tried this in my own life and in the lives of my children. In order to create a mindset of gratitude (you may have also heard the term "abundance") you state three things that you are grateful for. It's a basic exercise that can be done in your head or aloud with others, as I do with my family. Just think of it as the little bit of time before Thanksgiving where everyone goes around the table and states something they are thankful for. If you've never done this in your family, and growing up I don't think I did, think about a time you may have intentionally been grateful for something. Gratitude produces positivity and a better outlook on life. If gratitude doesn't come naturally, build the habit of gratitude by focusing on intention through behavior.

We can tie this directly to the spiritual life. You can accept these virtues and work on them, but in order to have a true understanding of your place in life and why you should have gratitude, you must understand the Gospel of Jesus Christ. In the Christian Scriptures you find the oft-quoted phrase in Phil 4:6–7: "Do not worry about anything, but in everything by prayer and supplication with thanksgiving let your requests be made known to God. And the peace of God, which surpasses all understanding, will guard your hearts and your minds in Christ Jesus."[1] Furthermore, 1 Thess 5:18 states, ". . . give thanks in all circumstances; for this is the will of God in Christ Jesus for you."[2] Thanksgiving, which also might be read as gratitude, is a necessary feature of the Christian

---

1. Phil 4:6–7, NRSV.
2. 1 Thess 5:18, NRSV.

life. In addition to the scientific research supporting gratitude, it is a core element of a healthy spiritual life.

So where does that leave us? We've taken a step back and looked at our life as it really is. This gives us humility. From humility, we are brought to a place of gratitude—to learn to be thankful for the things we do have, while striving for the goals and character we wish to obtain. This has built a solid foundation of knowing who we are and where we are at in our current place in life. Without this knowledge, we cannot know what to do, because we would not know where we were starting from. In this way, the virtues we have been discussing build upon one another. Again, we can think of this as the three A's: first the virtues of *awareness*, then the virtues of *action*, and lastly, the virtues of *agreement*. With this in mind, we are now led to the first of the virtues of action, diligence.

5

Diligence

I N THE SEARCH TO apply these virtues to our lives, we need to focus on both cognitive thought and action. With diligence, we move to active virtues in our path to building character. To recap, we started with virtues of awareness (humility and gratitude), now move to virtues of action (diligence and agency), and finish with virtues of agreement (forgiveness, relationship, and kindness). Now that we have moved into the action stage of virtue development, we can begin to actually work on our current situation. Diligence is the key.

Diligence means working hard and continuing to grind when you don't feel like it. Don't confuse this with overworking. There must be rest and time for prayer and meditation. In order to stay diligent, you must also rest. In fact, I would go so far as to say that deliberate rest, including prayer and meditation, is included in the intention of diligence. In other words, you must be diligent at resting in the same way you are diligent at working. Diligence is about intention and following through on that intention. Just as we must be intentional about our humility and our gratitude (as well as all virtues), we must be intent on being diligent in the many endeavors we undertake, both in our broader goals and in our everyday life activities such as eating, sleeping, and entertainment. There are three concepts that go with this. First, diligence must emerge from the virtues of awareness. Second, the intention to be diligent is a habit that must be formed, like all virtues. Third, diligence must be balanced and continual.

As we started out saying, diligence must *first* emerge from humility and gratitude, the virtues of awareness. Diligence without direction, knowledge, or wisdom becomes an exercise in futility. How many of you work hard yet get nowhere? If you have no direction to your work, no intention, you will not reap the rewards you seek. This is true in both achievement in your chosen career, and also in your character development. The good news is that if you already have a strong work ethic, even if misguided, you are far ahead of the person who has no work ethic, but some intention. Both are necessary, but if you already know how to work hard and be diligent, you only need point yourself in the right direction. This can be done through the process of humility and gratitude we have already spoken of. In that process, you have learned who you are in relation to God and humanity. Then, you looked inward to see what you should be spending your time on. Without this work of looking inward, we cannot know where to go.

Diligence is the *action* of this internal work. If you do not have diligence, the work of gratitude and humility is wasted. In the Gospels Jesus tells us, "If you love me, you will keep my commandments" (John 14:15), and the book of James tells us that ". . . just as the body without the spirit is dead, so faith without works is also dead" (Jas 2:26).[1] In the Christian Scriptures the movement is always from inward to outward. The intention/belief of a person's heart is borne out in action. If you say you are humble and want to reach your goals, the diligence you activate as a result of your humility and gratitude is the proof or action of that intention. If we do not act on the newfound beliefs and character we have obtained in our awareness of ourselves, we go nowhere. Even further we are not demonstrating the change in character and mindset that we seemingly have accepted. In the book of James, it speaks about

1. John 14:15 and Jas 2:26, NRSV.

faith being dead without works. This is a misunderstood passage for many Christians because the rest of the New Testament focuses on the grace of God and how we are saved by faith, not works. But James makes clear that without works, faith is not true faith. The point being made here is that the actions that flow from your belief prove your belief to be true. It's not that you need to earn your salvation, it is that your salvation projects your need to act in light of that salvation. Starting with works does not earn grace, but once you have experienced grace, it will lead to good works showing in your life. In the same way, our diligence flows out of our humility, our gratitude. We are diligent and work toward our goals because we now have clear goals and must work toward them. If we have goals but do not work at them, are they really goals? Or are they just distant wishes? The mindset (and action) of diligence is the natural virtue of acting out our goals reached in humility and gratitude. We are aware of who we are, where we are, and where we need to go. Diligence is the path to reaching that place, whether in a career or in character development.

Second, diligence must be both an intention and a habit that is formed. Diligence doesn't just happen. Just as we have been intentional about the virtues of awareness, we must be intentional about the virtues of action, starting with diligence. Though our diligence flows from the virtues of awareness, we must continually work on it. This is the "secret" that many people do not grasp: without continual focus on your virtues, your character, and your actions, they will slip away. Strong habit forming will do much good, but if it is not maintained, unfortunately our lives are like the second law of thermodynamics—they tend toward destruction. Being diligent means setting forth a plan to work every day and following that plan. I used to think that this kind of structure was limiting. I wanted to be free to go where the day took me. Freedom is very important, but if you do not choose a structure to follow, you will not be free. You will be at the whim of your emotions, the very thing you are trying to appease in the first place. The bottom line is that if you do not control your emotions, your schedule, your work habits, then they will be controlled for you. Freedom is choosing to take control of your time and decisions. You are not a slave to a structure; you have chosen that structure. If it isn't working for you, you can choose another structure/schedule/goal/ whatever you want. If your base virtues are set properly, you will see where you need to go. Diligence is the step of going there.

This is an important realization for the reaching of our goals. You have to have a plan to reach those goals, whether it be spiritually or materially. Some people are fortunate to have done this implicitly, but for many people, it must be done explicitly. From there, explicit habits become implicit ones, and you will do things because you are in the habit of doing them. They will feel natural and normal because you have trained yourself to do such. Diligence leads to the feeling of freedom because you will go to sleep every night knowing that you have not betrayed your own goals and duties. This type of peace is far more valuable than a perceived freedom lost to outside forces. By trying to be "free" you have chosen slavery; you have taken the ability to choose what to do with your time out of your hands. And if you do this well, down the road you will have the perceived freedom you desire because less time will be needed to do the things that will make you successful, both in your inner and outer life.

To push this a bit further, for those of us who have created an inner character built on honesty, we are conflicted when we make poor choices. If you know what is right and what your goals are, every step you take against those goals is a betrayal of your inner self. You have decided that spending that money, eating that food, staying up late and watching that TV show is more important than your long-term goal. Internally you know this is not true, so when you do this, you know you are lying to yourself for short-term gain. And let's be honest, you probably know that it's not even a short-term gain, but some kind of coping mechanism. Building long-term character to achieve spiritual and material goals requires diligence. It requires the building of habit, and habit is formed through repeated action. You must start with little steps and build to bigger ones. Unfortunately, our culture has told us that we can become famous overnight, can get rich quick, and will be popular immediately. Those things can and do happen in the short-term, but if you are on the long-term path, you can be pleasantly surprised when they happen versus biding time for something that will never happen. This will lead to regret, and again, this stems from the betrayal you feel. You might project this betrayal on others or you might say it "wasn't meant to happen," but how can you know this if you never take the steps to move yourself toward completion? Diligence is central to this. I dislike the old adage, but it rings true: the answer to the question, "how do you eat an elephant?" is "one bite at a time." You cannot get it all at once, and often getting it all at once is problematic. That's why those with quick fame or individuals who win the lottery waste their good fortune. They didn't take the proper steps to achieve it, so they don't know what to do with it. Stay the course, build your virtue, and *be diligent*. All of this flows from intention. Intention leads to action, and action is carried out through diligence. It also connects directly to the next virtue we'll look at—*agency*.

If we take this a step further and connect directly to times of unexpected difficulty, it focuses our diligence (and our agency) further because there are limitations to what we can do in the midst of trial. We may not be able to work on the normal projects that fill our time. Instead of thinking of this in a negative way, think of it as an opportunity. Without the clutter of what we "should" do, from the perspective of those around us, we can work on what we "need" to do. We have more space to step away and write the things we need to write, think about the things we need to think about, and create the things we need to create. Whether this be something tangible, like a birdhouse, a garden, a chair, or something ethereal like a concept, a formula, or a theory, we can control our time and space more easily. We can cut out poor influences and take back control of our time. With the virtue of diligence, we can build habits that can then be carried forward when things are "back to normal." Tangibly, if you are in a situation where you feel you cannot get things done during stressful times, use the time to rest, meditate, and recuperate yourself. Again, set things in order so that you are rested and ready for the next step when things get back to "normal."

What about during those "normal" times? What if things seem good overall, but your life is cluttered with unnecessary tasks and thoughts? It may be incumbent upon you to create your own space. You may have to make some hard decisions to cut out destructive, or even neutral, influences in your life. You might have to reset your schedule to your goals and needs. This is a hard thing to do, and one of the reasons we stay stuck in bad habits. The benefit of a time of extreme trial is that some of these changes have been forced upon us and we can act in accordance with the reality of the situation. If you are not working on your character during a time of extreme difficulty then you must create the urgency and space yourself (and be thankful that the difficulty isn't forced on you). That said, if you have already taken the steps of humility and gratitude and can see your path clearly, it follows that you will be able to take this next step of diligence. The hard part of lifting the veil of false expectations has been done. Being diligent is just the natural progression of acting on what you already know to be true.

6

Agency

DILIGENCE IS KEY TO exerting effort toward your goals, and the amount of diligence you can apply is directly proportional to the amount of *agency* you have. If you have agency, you know where your diligence can be put to use. Understanding that diligence flows from humility and gratitude is the basis of agency. It is the cognitive knowledge that you *can* do certain tasks, while there are other things you cannot do. This could be because you are not able; they are out of your control. It could also be that you cannot do them because your moral center, your character, will not allow you to do those things. I know that I could be a much wealthier person if I was willing to cut some ethical corners. That is not to say that I cannot become wealthy, or that I cannot make money, but having particular ethics in place prevents me from certain actions that might result in wealth. That said, were I to pursue wealth by unethical means, I might give up something much more valuable in the pursuit of that wealth.[1] The point is that agency is

1. This does not mean that we should not build wealth, especially for the right reasons. However, it does mean it should be done ethically and with good stewardship in mind. People tend to misunderstand this and pursue wealth for selfish ends, or avoid wealth altogether, thinking it is an evil. It is not an evil in itself, but love of wealth causes evil (1 Tim 6:10).

the virtue that centers us in the realization of what we are able and unable to do. It follows from humility and gratitude, just like diligence. In writing this text, I could have led with either diligence or agency because they are inextricably tied together. Understanding the agency under your control frees you to continue on the road to good character and career goals.

So, what is agency? It seems like an odd term to connect to virtue. I doubt you've read about virtues in the past or even thought about them randomly and said, "Hmmm, agency seems like it should be at the top of that list." In fact, I'm guessing it wouldn't be on the list at all. So, part of my job is to argue for its inclusion. That starts with a definition. With that in mind: agency is the ability that one has to create or decide their actions; it is the freedom one has to do things. So, should agency be a virtue? I would argue in the context of our discussion that yes, it should be, but with that comes some context. Agency in itself is the mode by which we can decide to build our character and virtues, while diligence is the action of building them. Agency ties in closely to the concept of intention. In the context of our text, think of it this way: first we focus on humility, which tells us who we are and our place in the order of things. Second, we focus on gratitude, which sets our mind right and solidifies our place in the world, and in relation to God and others. This includes an intention dedicated to setting our attitude correctly. Third, we move to agency/diligence, which are two sides of the same coin. Agency is the awareness of our freedom that emerges from humility and gratitude, and diligence is the acting out of it. If humility/gratitude pair together as an understanding of our place in relation to God and other humans, with humility the initial realization and gratitude a tangible action that connects to it, agency/diligence pair together with agency being the knowledge of our freedom and diligence the actions connected to it. Starting with diligence might be natural because it is more familiar, and is an easier "sell" as a virtue. However, without agency, diligence never comes to be. It is inextricably tied to diligence because it is the conceptual awareness of our freedoms. Without this conceptual awareness, diligence cannot be managed properly, i.e., it has no proper direction.

How does this work? We approach agency as an awareness, leading to intention of our freedoms. This is not just the realization that you are openly free and can do whatever you like. It is also the awareness that you have limitations, whether imposed by nature, imposed by circumstances, or imposed by your own character (or decisions). Understanding agency is understanding not just your place in the universe, as with humility and gratitude, but understanding your place in regard to your goals and intentions. When you reach the step of agency, you are ready to act in diligence, but you also have an understanding of what actions are available to you at a given time. This does not mean that certain actions will be unavailable later; it only means you know what you *can* do at a given time. Just like a game of chess, where only particular moves are available at any given point in a game, you can only apply diligence to individual actions depending on the amount of freedom you have at a given time. But also like chess, those earlier moves (actions) set up later actions, and so even if you are not "free" to do something at a particular time, it does not mean that the actions you are free to do are not working toward that future action. We could look at this financially. In an extremely simple example, a child might not have enough money to buy a candy bar, which costs one dollar. But if that child receives an allowance of twenty-five cents per week, in four weeks, they will have the freedom to buy that candy bar.[2] However, if they do not save the twenty-five cents each week, they will continue to lack the freedom to commit that particular action. Just as four decisions to save will result in the freedom to act in buying the candy bar, our decisions at each point in life add up to "unlock" available freedoms. Typically, this is more complex than a candy bar (if only it were that simple!), but the principle is the same. Imagine hundreds of choices that must be made properly to unlock a particular set of freedoms and enhance

2. Of course this does not take into account sales tax, which I learned at an early age as I tried to pay for the two-for-a-dollar toy cars I chose and didn't have the tax. Obviously, this lesson stuck with me.

one's agency. Our goal is to simplify this as much as possible, yet at the same time, making strong decisions at each encounter will enhance our agency, and hence our ability to be diligent to work toward a new goal.

Staying with the candy bar example, we can see how diligence and agency work hand-in-hand. If we are not diligent in following our initial choice to save twenty-five cents, we will not have the agency we desire to be diligent in saving the next twenty-five cents, and eventually in taking the action of purchasing the candy bar. *Agency leads to diligence, and diligence leads to more agency.* This is a fully symbiotic relationship that builds both our character and our freedom. In this way, agency is not a typical virtue, but a responsibility in itself. Allow me to explain. Because agency and diligence are symbiotic, they are both necessary in working toward goals—more so for temporal goals. However, you might make the case for spiritual goals also if you look at agency as a reservoir of internal strength. As this agency grows, one's responsibility grows. There is more power held by the individual. So, we could quote Spider-Man and say, "With great power comes great responsibility," which is true, but since we're grounded a bit more spiritually we might prefer to go to the biblical text: "From everyone to whom much has been given, much will be required; and from the one to whom much has been entrusted, even more will be demanded."[3] As we grow our agency through our diligence, we gain more and more power and ability. With this gain, we also have more responsibility and are entrusted with this power. This is another reason that humility and gratitude are essential building blocks of diligence/agency. Without this formed character, we are unable to handle the greater agency/freedom responsibly. This is why it is important to first build a foundation for power, wealth, responsibility, or most other things you wish to acquire in life. The same is true of character, though these go hand in hand. If you try to gain power quickly, or become wealthy fast, you may fail. As I mentioned in the past chapter, this is why lottery winners or those

---

3. Luke 12:48b, NRSV

who experience quick fame often fail.[4] They have not built up the proper agency to act in a manner befitting of their newfound status. Without virtue, without character, without this foundation, the weight of responsibility that comes with this new agency fails.

Let's take the example of the lottery winner, or someone who comes into money quickly. If they do not understand what it normally takes to acquire that kind of wealth, they also do not understand how to maintain it. Spider-Man teaches us that "with great power comes great responsibility," but by that same token, with great responsibility comes great power. The more people/things/institutions you are responsible for, the more power you hold over the success of those things. This is something we often forget. We want the power, and we want the quick agency, but we do not have the internal power/agency to control the external responsibility we now hold. This is also why if you work to build your character and your goals in a systematic way, they will prepare you for the newfound power and responsibility that may come to you. You don't know when it will come or how it will come. It may go according to plan or it may not, but if you have been systematically building your character along with your business/education/trade/relationships, then you will be (at least somewhat) prepared for the success and responsibility that is thrown your way. In fact, I might argue that this is proportional in most cases. The opportunities given to you are scalable to the character that you display to those around you. This isn't to say that you get everything you "deserve" immediately. Remember that humility requires that we don't follow a road of entitlement.

Taking this discussion to the spiritual realm, that is why it is essential to have a strong spiritual life. It keeps us humble; it keeps us grateful. If we see ourselves in the light of an omnipotent, just God we can know that as "good" or "talented" as we are, we fall far short. We also know that we commit evil in many ways that may only be known to us, but are present nonetheless. Keeping

---

4. We also see this in the stock market or the housing market when prices go up too quickly. The price accelerates faster than the value. A foundation of value (or in our case character) provides sustainable growth.

this humble attitude allows us to continue to be more and more responsible in light of the larger amounts of agency we receive as a result of our diligence.

In conclusion, agency is a virtue and a commodity. It grows with us and is both responsibility and power. Agency is the reservoir of action that diligence both flows out of and grows from. Diligence creates agency, and agency creates more powerful diligence. Acquiring agency without diligence leads to poor management of our agency, and is self-defeating. In order to keep growing our influence, power, and ability, we must be diligent and tend to our agency like a gardener in the garden. If we do not, we will soon lose that agency because we have no control over it. Intention, thus, is an important part of maximizing one's agency because intention leads to diligence which leads to agency.

7

Relationship

ONE OF THE THINGS I stated initially is that expectations change in times of extreme stress. This is true in our responsibilities and accomplishments, but it is also true in one other essential area of our lives: relationships. Some of us thrive on relationships, needing constant human contact, while others prefer to be alone much of the time. Whichever camp you fall into, relationship is a central part of our lives as human beings. Relationships fall into three categories, which we will revisit further in the next couple of chapters: relationship with God, relationship with other humans, and relationship with oneself. This threefold approach to relationship is true when talking about forgiveness, and also when speaking of kindness/love. To put it under our larger umbrella, relationship, forgiveness, and kindness all fall under the category of virtues of *agreement*, virtues that connect us to God, others, and ourselves.

To review, the first group of virtues, humility and gratitude, are in the grouping of *awareness*—they help us to know our place in the universe. Second, the virtues of diligence and agency fall under the grouping of *action*—virtues that create our direction and power in life. Lastly, relationship, forgiveness, and kindness (love), all fall under the heading of *agreement*—virtues that help us to get along with others in this life. This last category of virtues is essential because we are in relationship with others whether we want to be or not. Even if we are somehow able to avoid all other humans, you will never escape God or yourself. You will always have to deal with those two entities.

I present relationship as a similar virtue to agency. It is not typically thought of as a virtue, and perhaps in this case it might be better seen as a category that encompasses other virtues. Either way, I want us to look at proper relationships with others as a core virtue in our lives and on our path to accomplishing the spiritual and secular goals on which we are working. Relationships work in tandem with forgiveness and kindness. This is extremely important because in our current society it has become normal for people to talk about toxicity and cutting "toxic relationships" out of our lives. While I do think that choosing the relationships you enter (and exit) and the degree to which you are involved with people is important, you must make sure that you are holding up your end of the bargain, so to speak. It is not enough to have a bunch of "yes men" friends tell you to leave someone behind or to ghost them—an idea that should rarely be acted on with those you are in true relationship with, except perhaps in cases of abuse. Because it has become so easy to jump into relationship with others due to social media and a culture of instant communication, it is also much easier to jump out of relationship.

Let's start there by talking about social networks and relationships. As I mentioned in the introduction, as I discussed the work of Albert Borgmann and Hubert Dreyfus, relationships in an online environment are less than they are in the "real world." As Dreyfus mentions, there is less risk and commitment, which makes us avoid having a real relationship.[1] So, it has become much easier for us to jump in and out of relationships, and we are never fully invested in them. This can lead to a lot of hurt feelings and consummation of what I would term "empty calories," relationships

1. "Social Networking and Ethics."

that feed us but are never enough because they offer little sustenance. There is no "nutrition" in these types of relationships.

As I mentioned previously, truth is the foundation for all of our virtues. Honesty and truth allow everything else to flourish. If you cannot be honest with yourself, others, and God, you will never truly be a person of character. If you cannot be trusted, you have failed. Sometimes this is out of our control, but we must be certain that we are controlling the things in our purview. Relationships are a great indicator of this. You may not have perfect relationships with others, but you can be a good coworker, friend, spouse, etc. by strengthening your own character through a foundation of honesty and truth. Imagine in our current political climate if we could be certain that those who disagree with us had a common love of truth. That would help to alleviate the strong mistrust we currently feel for one another. Truth connects us in a way that builds trust and relationship. If we could share the virtue of truth, then our relationships would follow from a place of security. We still may not want to invest our time with everyone we see, but we would know that it was possible. This is why every time you lie, whether it be large or small, you erode trust, which is the very foundation of all relationships. You cannot expect others to be truthful when you have created so many exceptions to truth in your own heart. And I suspect that you also might be more willing to trust if you knew that you yourself were trustworthy. Dishonesty breeds dishonesty. However, I can tell you, as someone who does do his best to tell the truth, that you will see dishonesty around you all the time. But what truth-telling does do is make you more attune to lies. It goes back to that old adage that in order to spot a counterfeit, you need to know the real thing inside and out. You won't always be able to know every permutation of lie that is out there, but if you know what is true, you can spot the lie by comparing it to the truth. Knowing yourself (stemming from humility and gratitude), and acting on it (diligence and agency), puts you in a position to have healthy and strong relationships because you are confident in who you are and in knowing who other people are.

Relationship

Like agency, relationship is not really a traditional virtue, but perhaps it should be. Typically, we look at the virtues within relationships, let's say kindness, sharing, honesty, etc. But by creating a virtue of relationship, we are stating that we value relationships. We are saying that relationships are essential to our very essence as a human being. Relationships influence us in a multitude of ways, and are influenced by us. By creating a foundation of character, we become the major influencer in a relationship, not the one influenced. Notice that I said "major influencer." It is not that you cannot be influenced, but the influence toward you will be lessened, at least in negative terms. Ideally, when both parties are of strong moral character, they will only influence each other in a positive way because the virtue of character in each of them is keeping the negative at bay. This is related to the necessity of relationships; relationship is a virtue because it is a part of who we are. We do not accept that we should jump in and out of relationships willy-nilly, but take them seriously. To be in relationship is virtuous, and we can expand that to include relationship with God and with ourselves. We might even expand it to animals and other forms of nature. Relationship is a virtue that must be tended to by other virtues, and the foremost of these are forgiveness and kindness (love).

Furthermore, the importance of relationship flows down from the Christian concept of the Trinity. God is a relational God and a personal God.[2] God in three persons is also relational within the Godhead. The Father, Son, and Holy Spirit are in relationship with one another, while also being in relationship with humanity. God's loving relationship with us is a model for our relationship with others. God is not influenced negatively by human actions, just as a virtuously formed human (ideally), is not influenced negatively by the actions of others. This may not be an ideal reached in this lifetime, but it is a model of it. In this same way, the relationship between the Godhead may point to a healthy internal relationship with ourselves. This is something I would like to ponder more, but

2. Again, this may be seen in other religious traditions, but it is my belief that it is best experienced through relationship with the God of Christianity through his Son Jesus Christ.

perhaps, at the least it is a model for the family and marriage and the sacredness of each. Because relationship is such a central part of the Godhead and of our own network of life, it makes perfect sense to list it among these essential virtues.

Just as diligence breeds agency, which breeds diligence, which breeds more agency, relationship breeds forgiveness and kindness, and forgiveness and kindness breed relationship. These two essential parts of our lives, agency and relationship, live in symbiosis (let's say relationship) with other cardinal virtues, thus making them both nontraditional virtues but also core virtues. You might envision the virtues in this book sort of like this:

Awareness: (humility and gratitude) → Action:

(diligence ←→ agency) → Agreement:

(Relationship ←→(Forgiveness and Kindness))

These virtues both build and interact with each other in ways that make them all essential to living a full life, but are not isolated or linear. If we look at these virtues as a whole, we will see that we must continually reestablish them in our lives, lest the whole system start to fail. Why am I mentioning this in a chapter on relationship? First, what better place to do it? The relationship between virtues also mirrors our relationship with other people, ourselves, and God. In the next chapter on forgiveness, I'll lay out the relationship of guilt and forgiveness to these three categories, but as I've alluded to, these are the three types of relationships in our lives between persons. Second, as we have moved into the last category of virtues, agreement, it is a good place to show how the whole system of virtues in this book connect to each other. So, what we'll see is that relationship is ultimately built on love and forgiveness and that the practice of these virtues within relationships will make them stronger and result in potentially more (healthy) relationships. And guess what? If you are humble, grateful, and diligent within those relationships, you'll be able to exercise love and forgiveness for both yourself and the one with whom you are in relationship.

What we see in this approach to life is that virtues are often simple, yet hard to exercise. Everyone wants a magic path to success, whether it be in relationships, their career, or their spiritual life, and the fact of the matter is that though things are simple and straightforward, they are not easy. We have to be willing to put in the work and focus on what matters. We see this in the building of habit in ancient philosophy and early Christianity. The way that the church fathers built their spiritual life is the same way you were told to do so in your twentieth (and hopefully twenty-first) century Sunday school classes as a child. Remember the song: "Read your Bible, pray every day, and you'll grow, grow, grow."?[3] Funny enough that's the same foundation that early Christians used to prepare for the trials of life. And even still, the spiritual life is built on reading Scripture and praying, which are the foundations of building humility and all of the virtues we're discussing. Just do the work, be humble, and healthy relationships will follow.

So, what of relationship? Despite the way that society has compartmentalized and psychologized relationships, both in person and through social media, they are an essential part of our lives and flow from our own character formation. If you are the person you want to be, you will have better relationships. Yes, sometimes that means setting boundaries or cutting people out of your lives, but this should be done in love and with forgiveness. We'll talk about those in the next two chapters. We also must treat people with respect online as well as in person. If your habits in day-to-day social media are to demonize, disrespect, and mock others, perhaps what you are doing in real life is either a façade or reflected in what you do online. Or is it the other way around? The success you wish to have in life is rooted in your own virtue and character, and this is rooted in honesty, and ultimately God. Relationships are both a reflection and a reservoir of these virtues. Be wise in who you befriend, but also be wise in how you treat *all* people.

---

3. "Read Your Bible, Pray Every Day," *Children's Bible Songs*. Although this is a common Sunday school song going back many years, its origins are a bit murky.

8

Forgiveness

C ONGRATULATIONS! YOU'VE REACHED ONE of the most important chapters in this text. If I were to choose two virtues that are essential to our lives, yet the hardest to practice, this would be the second one. If you hadn't figured it out, the first one is humility. Why are these two virtues so hard to practice? The answer is that both require one to be honest with themselves and others, and to *perhaps* lower themselves from the imaginary pedestal that they have placed themselves on. Again, honesty is the foundation for all of these virtues, but especially the hard ones. But why specifically is forgiveness so hard? And what does forgiveness entail? In this chapter we look at a few different aspects of forgiveness. First, we answer the question of why forgiveness is so difficult. We all struggle with forgiving others and being forgiven. Second, we look at the different types of forgiveness—both ontological (I'll explain what that means) and practical. I'll also break down the three types of practical forgiveness (relationship with God, others, and self). These three types break both ways and are worth understanding. Third, I'll present the cycle of forgiveness and why it is important to complete this cycle.[1] This chapter will be a bit longer than some

1. These divisions are mine, and I feel they are the most helpful way to

of the other chapters on virtue due to the necessary details, but it is important to get a full picture of forgiveness, which, as I said, is one of the two most difficult virtues to enact.

WHY IS FORGIVENESS SO HARD?

We all struggle with forgiving others, and this is a very difficult part of life. On the other hand, we all want to be forgiven instantly, don't we? I would argue part of the reason we have trouble forgiving others is because we have trouble both forgiving ourselves and accepting forgiveness from others. In fact, sometimes it seems the harder part of forgiveness is accepting it, rather than giving it. I am guessing if many of you reading this book are like me, it is hard to forgive yourself because you hold yourself to a high standard. That might be why you're reading a book like this in the first place—because you care. That caring also leads you to take your wrongdoings seriously, which makes you vulnerable to rejecting offered forgiveness. If this is the case, then you might feel you deserve to feel guilty, revisiting your wrongdoings and mistakes over and over again. In this way, you are both punishing yourself for things that you have been forgiven of (wrongdoings) and probably beating yourself up for things you don't need forgiveness from (mistakes). You'll notice that I separate wrongdoings and mistakes. Wrongdoings are things that you did that are clearly wrong and you know that you need to be forgiven from. Mistakes are things that may or may not have been wrong, but resulted in something you felt was unfavorable. Sometimes it feels good to be forgiven for the latter, but we should always seek forgiveness for the former. There are two reasons I make this distinction. First, so that we do not feel guilty for accidents for which we had no control. There's no benefit in feeling guilty for actions that could not have been changed. Again, sometimes forgiveness *might* be appropriate, but that is more to make sure a relationship is restored than to actually forgive wrongdoing. Second, and this is probably more

---

categorize what have been longstanding ways of understanding forgiveness in a theological and relational framework.

important to character formation, we must distinguish mistakes from wrongdoing because often people like to talk about their actions as mistakes, or accidents, while not owning up to the fact that it was actually wrongdoing. It is hard to receive forgiveness without admitting the wrong you have done. It is possible, but then you are not able to complete the cycle of forgiveness, which we'll talk about in a little bit. So when we struggle with receiving forgiveness, often it is an unwillingness to admit a wrongdoing, or a willingness to accept that someone else is able to forgive that wrongdoing.

On the other hand, some people struggle with offering forgiveness. There could be a multitude of reasons for this, but I think one of them is a lack of humility or kindness, both of which are discussed in this text. Matthew 18:21–35 sheds some light on this situation. In this parable, Jesus recounts a man who was forgiven ten-thousand talents, but then does not forgive a man who owes him a hundred denarii. The point Jesus is making is that you should forgive as you have been forgiven. If you've been forgiven much, why would you not forgive little things? This is why the framing of these virtues with truth and humility is so essential. If you see yourself as forgiven of your sin, why would you not forgive others who have sinned? Perhaps some feel that by holding off on forgiveness they are able to hold power over another person. This is very misguided. By forgiving you are letting go of the control that this wrongdoing holds over you also. Whether you are being forgiven or forgiving another, the act of forgiveness frees both parties from the wrongdoing and the continued harm that this wrongdoing will have over both of their lives. There is no limit to forgiveness. Though there may be consequences for wrongdoing not alleviated by forgiveness, in some cases legal, it is incumbent upon us to continue to forgive. As the famous phrase, found in verse twenty-two, speaks of how often to forgive: "Jesus said to him, 'Not seven times, but, I tell you, seventy-seven times.'"[2] We should not limit our forgiveness, but continually forgive others.

In a similar way, Luke 7:36–50 teaches us about forgiveness. While at dinner at a Pharisee's house Jesus asks who will love more,

2. Matt 18:22, NRSV.

the person who has been forgiven fifty or five-hundred denarii. Clearly the answer is the latter. In offering forgiveness to others, remember to keep in mind how much you have been forgiven. This is a part of humility—understanding things as they are. You might not hold the Christian Scriptures as an authority, but whether one is a Christian or not, the concept of forgiveness is basic to most approaches to virtue and the wisdom of the New Testament text still applies. Basically, whether you struggle with forgiving others or being forgiven, you must learn to let go of that mindset—as well as the wrongdoing you hold as so important. Forgiveness is a powerful tool and a virtue we must all master in order to live a free and full life.

THE TWO TYPES OF FORGIVENESS

Rooted in this idea of forgiveness and humility flowing down from God is also the concept of the two types of forgiveness: ontological and practical. Let's start with ontological.

Ontological Forgiveness

This may be a word that many of you are unfamiliar with, so let me define it and then leave it behind. Ontological, according to Merriam-Webster, is "relating to or based upon being or existence."[3] When we use this word in a theological context, it is connected to the essence of someone or something. In this case, ontological forgiveness is forgiveness of the very soul of a person. It is not forgiving someone for a particular wrongdoing, but forgiveness as a state of being. To put this a bit more simply, ontological forgiveness is the forgiveness that one receives through Jesus Christ for their sin. It is a new state of being that the Christian embraces once accepted into the family of God. Ontological forgiveness takes place because Jesus Christ, as both fully human and fully divine, serves as a mediator between humans and God, taking on this ontological sin

3. "Ontological," *Merriam-Webster*.

for all of us. Our status before God (our being) is changed by this forgiveness. This is truly the wellspring of all forgiveness.

This is why ontological forgiveness is an important concept for this text. In practice, you may not use this type of forgiveness, but understanding that you have been (or can be) forgiven of your wrongdoing in the very nature of your humanity frees us to practice the second type of forgiveness—practical forgiveness. Embracing ontological forgiveness allows you to practice proper humility and gratitude, which is the source of forgiveness. The deep well of ontological forgiveness continually centers us and allows us to practice practical forgiveness, which is an essential virtue of living a fulfilled, successful life.

Practical Forgiveness

That brings us to practical forgiveness. Practical forgiveness is the forgiveness that we typically think of in our everyday lives. It is practical. It is pragmatic. Someone wrongs you and you decide to forgive them. It's the forgiveness that Jesus is speaking of in the Gospels when he says to forgive someone "seventy-seven" times. And just like in the words of Jesus, that forgiveness is rooted in ontological forgiveness. Just as God the Father has forgiven you, you are to forgive others. Unlike in the parable of the servant who did not forgive after being forgiven much, the fruit of practical forgiveness is that you forgive *because* you have been forgiven much.

We must forgive others because it frees us from the prison of long-term anger and bitterness. We also must forgive because it restores relationships. You might forgive in order to let go of something minor you've been holding on to for years, which causes damage to your own psyche. This might be related to someone you will never see again, so why hold on to it? Forgive them and move on. It also might be because someone you have a close relationship with wronged you and you need to restore that relationship. It could be with family, friends, or an acquaintance. It might result in that relationship being forever minimized in some way—forgiving, but moving on. It might also result in a full restoration of a relationship that you either cannot or do not want to end. Forgiveness works. Let God decide the fate of the wrongdoer. You might say, as I sometimes do, that "that isn't fair," or "what about justice?" Again, justice is for God to decide. This does not mean you let someone take advantage of you or put you back in a harmful relationship. That is when forgiving and moving on is helpful. I'll leave it to you to decide what form the relationship takes moving forward. Just make sure that on your end you have forgiven and let it go. You cannot control what others do. Forgiveness is one of the most powerful things you can do for both yourself and others. It is also something that you can fully control on your own end. Others may not reciprocate that forgiveness or accept that forgiveness, but that's not the point. It's obviously better if they do, which I'll talk about in a minute. But don't let their unwillingness to forgive prevent you from doing what you know is right, and what will be best for both you and them.

To break it down even further, there are three relationships in which forgiveness can be exercised, and they run both ways (forgiver and the one being forgiven), though it may not seem like that at first: forgiveness between God and humans, forgiveness between humans and humans, and forgiveness between you and yourself. Let's look at each one briefly.

Practical Forgiveness Between God and Humanity

Before we engage in forgiveness between ourselves and others, we must revisit the forgiveness between God and humanity. The relationship between God and humanity is the one relationship that exercises both ontological and practical forgiveness. We see this arrangement woven throughout the Christian Scriptures, and can find some similarities in other religious traditions. The root of all forgiveness is the ontological forgiveness that God gives to humans in a relationship with Jesus Christ. Once this has been established, your ontological state of sin has been eliminated. You are no longer a child of sin, but a child of God. However, like any good parent-child relationship, the child still disobeys the parent.

Even though a state of being that is free from sin is applied to a person, they are still prone to wrongdoing. It is for this wrongdoing that we must be offered forgiveness.

In a state of practical forgiveness between God and humans, humans (we) do wrong, we ask for forgiveness, and God forgives us. It is a clear transaction. The oft-quoted 1 John 1:9 lays this out clearly: "If we confess our sins, he who is faithful and just will forgive us our sins and cleanse us from all unrighteousness."[4] Just as ontological forgiveness cleanses our soul from the state of being of sin, practical forgiveness reinstalls the relationship between ourselves and God. It reconciles the wrongdoing between us. The act of us requesting forgiveness installs a sense of humility and acceptance, and God gives this forgiveness freely, based on the work of Jesus Christ.

Practical Forgiveness—Person to Person

In the same way, we must forgive one another and ask for forgiveness when we do wrongdoing. As I've mentioned previously, the forgiveness we give each other is rooted in this broader ontological forgiveness that is given by God. We forgive because we have been forgiven. In order to exercise this properly, we follow the cycle of forgiveness, which I will present in the next section. The person-to-person transaction of forgiveness is more complicated than the one between us and God. This is due to the fact that both parties must be willing participants in order for a full reconciliation to occur. If one party is willing to forgive, but the other does not accept, the relationship still has a problem. On the contrary, if one party humbles themselves and asks for forgiveness, but it is still not offered, we do not have full reconciliation because the wrongdoing has not been cleared in the relationship.

Because of the necessity of both parties to complete the action, person to person, for full reconciliation, both people must be willing and in a state of mind to do so. In this text, I am arguing that forgiveness is a necessary part of living a successful life, and

4. 1 John 1:9, NRSV.

the key to love and relationships. Therefore, you must make sure that whatever the other party's disposition, your disposition is one of forgiveness. Be sure to forgive when you are wronged, and to ask for, and receive, forgiveness when you have committed wrong. Again, this does not necessarily lead to a relationship continuing on in the same way. Sometimes a wrongdoing will break trust in an irreparable, or at least long-term, way. In those cases, I would still argue that you must forgive or be forgiven, then move on with wisdom as you go forward. Person to person forgiveness is essential to your well-being, the well-being of others, and of building a reputation of someone who is of strong, loving character.

Forgiveness Between You and Yourself

Okay, so this one is a bit tricky, but when you have committed wrong against another person, you need to forgive yourself. I think you could argue this comes last, after asking forgiveness from God and the person/group you wronged, but you do need to forgive yourself in order to move forward. Having strong character means doing the difficult things, and for some of us, it is easier to humble ourselves and ask forgiveness from a friend than it is to ask forgiveness of ourselves. Maybe better stated, the high bar that you have set for your character forces you to struggle with forgiving yourself for breaking your own standard.

There are a few ways to approach this. First, you might tell yourself that God has forgiven you, and if God is willing to forgive you, then how can you not forgive yourself? If the sinful disposition you have toward God and others has been forgiven, why would you not "follow God's lead" and forgive yourself? This makes logical sense if you accept that God has forgiven you. Second, you might go back to the focus of what we are doing in this book—trying to build character through virtue to live a full life. This might sound somewhat counterintuitive, but if you are going to exercise good character, it is not just following a set of rules. It is living in a virtuous way. In order to complete this virtue, you must forgive as well as be forgiven, and that includes forgiving yourself.

In these three types of practical forgiveness we see an underlying theme that should not be ignored. The reason you need to receive forgiveness from all three sources is because you have wronged all three parties, including yourself. You have broken your own standard. So, forgive yourself just as you would forgive your friend, just as that forgiveness comes from God's forgiveness of you.

THE CYCLE OF FORGIVENESS

The cycle of forgiveness is a way of showing how the process of practical forgiveness moves from wrongdoing to reconciliation. This process is the ideal in forgiveness, but for various reasons the cycle may end unfinished because it takes two parties, at least in the form of person to person forgiveness.

The cycle of forgiveness looks like this:

> Wrongdoing leads to Guilt, which leads to Confession, which leads to Amends, which leads to Forgiveness, which leads to Reconciliation, which leads back to Wrongdoing. . . .

What is happening here is a movement in which the ultimate goal is reconciliation. Forgiveness is the key virtue here, but the goal is reconciliation. Because relationships are such an important part of our humanity (including our relationship with God and ourselves), we must seek to restore those relationships. The cycle of forgiveness helps us do that. Remember that this is the ideal, and is not always possible.

First, there is wrongdoing, or some might say sin. You did something (we'll take this from your end since on the other end you are the one granting forgiveness), and you need reconciliation. If you didn't do anything wrong, you don't need forgiveness. So, let's assume you did something wrong. You were cruel to your friend, you were disrespectful, you lied, etc.[5] After wronging your friend, you start to feel guilty. Guilt, contrary to what many say, is not a

---

5. Of all the things you could do wrong, don't ever lie. It undermines all the virtues we've discussed. Honesty is foundational to good character.

bad thing. It is a natural prompt to encourage us to make right the wrongs we commit. False guilt is another story, or not being able to let go of your guilt, but guilt itself can be a very positive thing. So, you did something wrong and now you feel guilty. As a result of that guilt you go to your friend and confess the wrongdoing; you ask them for forgiveness. At this point, hopefully they will grant you forgiveness, but sometimes you may have to acknowledge your wrongdoing further by making amends. Let's say you were mean to your friend. In this case, he might forgive you and you can move on. But, let's say you stole something, or cheated someone. In that case, you would have to make amends to repay the debt you've created. There may be cases where your friend also forgives the debt, but it is something you do owe. Another example is if you shamed your friend in a public place, depending on the situation, you may have to apologize publicly to restore their honor. Each situation is different, but the general concept holds. After moving through all the necessary steps of accepting forgiveness and making amends (if necessary), you are reconciled. Hooray! You and your friend have restored your relationship. This euphoric feeling is very hard to replicate—which is why forgiveness is also important outside of the foundation to character. You will hurt yourself by holding on to guilt. It must be alleviated.

After all of this good work to restore your relationship, chances are you will wrong your friend again or they will wrong you. You are human; it will happen. This cycle may happen in a matter of seconds or it may take years depending on the parties involved and the seriousness of the wrongdoing. Whatever happens, however, do try to complete this cycle, whether you are wronged or the one who committed a wrong.

All that said, what if your friend will not forgive you? What if your friend died before you could ask for forgiveness? What if you lost contact? These are all unideal situations, but ones in which many of us find ourselves. Though they can range from undesirable to outright morbid, I would point us back to our responsibility in each situation. If your friend will not forgive you but you've done everything properly to restore the relationship, it is now out of your hands. Sometimes people need time, and sometimes they are unwilling to forgive. While this hurts deeply, it is out of your control. Control the things you can, and be sure you have not given them a reason to withhold forgiveness. Then know that you've done what you can and move on. If they come back to complete the cycle, all the better. Though you may feel regret, you can point back to the cognitive knowledge that you did everything you could. Pray for them and move forward.

But what if your friend died? In this difficult circumstance, whether you needed to be forgiven or to tell them they are forgiven, you must also move on and forgive yourself. If there is a circumstance you can pass that forgiveness on to or request forgiveness from a family member to make amends, that may be appropriate in certain instances but not in others. Sometimes it is best to move forward. These are very difficult situations even without these complications. Forgiveness takes humility. Sometimes even the act of forgiving another will take humility, not holding on to a wrongdoing in a display of power, but letting go and showing love. Forgive freely and do not hesitate to ask forgiveness. Just like humility, though many see this as a sign of weakness, it is a sign of strength. Being able to put yourself in a vulnerable position, knowing you will be able to handle whatever comes your way, is the sign of ultimate strength. At that point you are no longer concerned about how you appear to others, but are concerned with your own character and what is right. Over time, this will impress those around you more than false bravado. It's like something else we learn in life: if you are trying to be cool, you are not cool. Being cool is being confident in who you are and just doing it. Take that same approach to your own character.

In a nutshell, that is forgiveness. There is much more that can be written. It is a key theological and psychological concept. It connects and heals our relationships. Through this chapter I hope you can see its importance in the framework of virtue, and why it is at the center of relationships. With that in mind, it's time to move to the ultimate virtue: kindness (love).

9

Kindness

N OW THAT WE'VE WORKED through the first six virtues, things culminate with the seventh: kindness. I use the term kindness, but we are really talking about love. True kindness is love, as opposed to a show of false niceties. To be kind to someone is to show them love. So far, we've discussed humility and gratitude, diligence and agency, and forgiveness and relationship. If you look at the progression, you will see that it moves from inward virtues to outer ones. This is important. In following the model we see in Christianity, it is not the outer actions that are most important. Those actions are only a reflection of one's inner character. In the culminating virtue, love, we see both of these brought together. Love is an inner attitude, but also an action toward others. By maintaining an inner self that is strong and pure, we are able to spread that goodness outward, resulting in happiness and success for both ourselves and those around us. If you approach the world with humility, gratitude, and diligence, you are able to spread love to others and also express your inner fulfillment.

Let's focus on kindness specifically. You'll notice at times I use love and kindness interchangeably, and the reason is that the type of kindness we are discussing is not just being "nice" to someone, but actually caring about them and connecting with them. Unfortunately the term "nice" has been used in recent years to refer to an action of kindness that is disingenuous. People are nice, but not kind. Kindness, however, is doing what is best for another person by showing them love. Sometimes that may look direct, or even cruel, but it is with the other's best interests in mind. This leads us to the other side of the pendulum. While some pretend to be kind by being "nice," others pretend to be kind by being "truthful." Telling others the truth is a loving act, but it can be done in a way that is kind or in a way that is hurtful. If you are doing so in the manner of the latter, you're not really being kind. You might help that person, but you might also harm them. Delivery and method matter as much as action or words. Being kind is being loving. If you love someone, you will be kind to them.

Building on the virtue of relationship, we see that kindness is what fuels a relationship. Loving another through kindness will grow your connection by becoming an outreach of your inner character. Your virtue is now shared with another and that creates a broader virtuous relationship that makes you and those around you better. This follows from my statement above about inner virtues moving to outer ones. By fulfilling and expressing the virtue that you have established in your inner character, you are able to share that virtue with those around you through your reflected, outer character. Love encompasses both the inner and the outer virtues. It is an inner virtue in that it must flow in and from you, but outer in that it also is shown in your actions and words. When you show kindness to another person, or a group of people, you express your true character. People can see who you are in your acts of kindness. Through these acts, you show love and humility. You show gratitude for what you have and for those around you. Kindness through love is the ultimate expression of virtue. Without this expression, all the virtue that you have collected, all the character you have built, and your very self is not shared in its fullest culmination.

Now let's turn that on its head. What if you've chosen not to work on your inner character? What if you allow entitlement, greed, and pride to run the show? Well, the same thing is going to happen, only it's not going to be pretty. Instead of an outpouring of kindness and love to others that flows from your abundance of virtue and character, you'll be pouring out hate, bitterness, and selfishness. If you don't establish the virtues already mentioned in this book, you will struggle to be kind to others because the root of your character will still be rotten. Some of you might ask—what about the phrase "fake it till you make it?" I am really not a fan of this phrase because it infers that by trying to act in a way that is contrary to what you want, you are "faking it." While we might look at it this way, we might also break this down further. By making the decision to act in a way that is consistent with a character trait you wish to have, you have already cognitively decided to make it. You have already set the intention to make it. So, you are not faking it, you are working on building a habit, and habits lead to success and build character. But it's a lot harder to take this path because you will continually struggle against your desires. By building up a vast array of virtues to begin with, you will struggle with those desires less because you will be in the habit of seeking other things. It isn't that we won't continually fight our negative passions; we will. However, by building up virtue you can ensure that what naturally flows out of you is good and pure. So, whether you set the intention to love, or whether you set the intention to build up other virtues, they both originate from the virtue of truth—the virtue that is the foundation for all of our discussion in this text. To put it in simple terms: it is a lot easier to love in a full sense if you have already built up other virtues. Be truthful with yourself and you will be more humble, more diligent, and more kind.

Kindness should be an easier "sell" than some of the other virtues because it is engrained in us from a young age to be kind to others. This kindness flows from many cultural and religious traditions. As it states in the book of Ephesians, ". . . be kind to one another, tenderhearted, forgiving one another, as God in Christ has forgiven you."[1] This Bible verse encapsulates the three virtues of agreement: relationship, forgiveness, and kindness. We are

1. Eph 4:32, NRSV.

kind to others and forgive them because of God's forgiveness of us. Implicitly we care about relationships with others because of this same reason. Let's continue down that path. In the book of 1 Corinthians we see the classic Christian definition of love:

> Love is patient, love is kind. It does not envy, it does not boast, it is not proud. It does not dishonor others, it is not self-seeking, it is not easily angered, it keeps no record of wrongs. Love does not delight in evil but rejoices with the truth. It always protects, always trusts, always hopes, always perseveres. Love never fails. . . . [2]

Funny enough, the biblical definition of love follows a lot of what is being shared in this book. This was not intentional. When I started out, I had a framework in mind for the book, and when I got to this chapter I thought of this passage. And there it is, in large part laying out the concepts I had developed, only they had already been clearly developed many years ago. Maybe that shouldn't be a surprise, since the biblical message often mirrors the ancient philosophical one and vice versa. But let's look at the passage. We see that love is not boastful or proud; in other words it is humble. Love does not envy or seek the self; this might be interpreted as being grateful. It always perseveres; it is diligent. And ultimately it is kind, patient, and "keeps no record of wrongs." You might say it is kind and forgiving. This reading that has become cliché for many Christians (and beyond) across America gives us the very understanding of character and being a successful human person. This reiterates why it is important for us to cognitively take a step back and settle our inner character. It is important to meditate and pray. It is important to think deeply about wisdom literature such as this. The act of this inner meditation goes a long way to building the character necessary to create a strong self, and from there a strong community.

As I said above, this process starts inwardly and moves outward. Through this outward movement of love and kindness we are able to bless the community that we have built around us through

2. 1 Cor 13:4–8a, NIV.

relationship. In addition, we are able to bless a community beyond the one we have built with the people we come in contact with every day through our work, acquaintances, and incidental contact in our cities and towns. This brings us back to difficult times—the impetus for which I am writing this text.

During the most recent pandemic, we have created two major situations out of the same one (granted I am speaking about the inner self and our relationships, not economic and biological damage). First, many of us have learned to be fearful of our fellow man. We see people wearing masks or not wearing masks. We are told to stay away from others. We have dehumanized other human beings by covering faces and creating more distance.[3] It is a byproduct of the situation. So many have come to see the other as diseased, inhuman, and distant. This is not good for the inclination to be kind and build relationships. Second, we have had distance and time to think about ourselves. We are able to look inward and take time that we wouldn't have taken otherwise. It was a sort of forced meditative retreat. If you've used this time wisely, it has given you the opportunity to think on these virtues and build up your character. It has sent you on a path toward the appreciation of your fellow humans, seeking a day when you can be reunited in relationship and love. Maybe it has given you a disposition of gratitude and kindness. For many of us this pandemic has sent us on one of these two paths, and in many cases, myself included, both. This is a recent example, but any time of trial that creates distance will do the same thing. The dehumanization of the other is not a recent problem, but one that we need to be aware of in our own lives. It is impossible to love another when we have made them out to be subhuman. So, where do we go from here? I would encourage us to seek the latter path. The path of appreciation and reconciliation. Use times of trial to build your character, starting with humility and gratitude. You might find yourself being more loving when the trial subsides.

3. This isn't meant to be a commentary on the effectiveness of wearing a mask, which has become a huge point of division globally.

Times of difficulty do not necessarily create new moral problems. The problems of sin, selfishness, and evil have been around for thousands of years. Difficulty shines a light on our weaknesses and places in our lives that we've neglected. It is an opportunity to refocus our energy on what matters. It is a chance to build our character so that the next trial is much easier—so that our lives in times of both good and bad are the way we want them to be. In the last chapter, I'll wrap this up and overview what we've learned about the importance of these particular virtues for a meaningful life, and hence a meaningful community. We can look forward to this time of greater strength.

Before we move on to that discussion on community, let's look specifically at what it means to be kind. To be kind to another person or a community is not about playing nice. It's not about putting on a façade, which should be clear from our earlier discussion. It is about showing true concern for the well-being of the other. When we place this true concern into action, it typically will appear as kindness. Many people don't know what to do or how to act toward others. They might have good intentions but not know what to do. I know that intentions don't always work out, and sometimes they are destructive. However, if you have built a strong character, your intentions and actions will follow. I have tried to live my own life by being genuine and authentic toward others. When I don't do this, it produces guilt because it creates a barrier between myself and another person in our relationship (or potential relationship). This doesn't mean I act the same in every situation. It doesn't mean I don't use tools and talents at my disposal to communicate in different ways. But it does mean I try to set my intention and character and then act within it. Kindness—read love—is the ultimate expression of this.

It is because of this authentic expression that forgiveness and relationship are such an important part of this trio of virtues. I will fail in my attempt to be kind. You will too. But having a cognitive bedrock of virtue and relationship, while exercising the giving and receiving of forgiveness, allows us to continue to be strong in our love. It also gives us recourse when we do fail.

This is true within a friendship, a marriage, or with someone we are related to. An attitude of kindness and forgiveness creates a foundational safety and strength for relationships to flourish. This is just one reason why love and kindness are so important, but there's a bigger reason that supersedes this: we are built for love; love is the core virtue of our being.

Everyone craves love. They need love. It is impossible to be human without understanding our need to love and to be loved. It flows directly from the relational nature of our Creator as a Trinitarian God, but also our relation as created beings of that relational God. You don't have to accept this pretext to know that love is essential to our being, but it helps to contextualize it for those who do believe in this God. There are two bookend virtues that encapsulate all of what I have been doing in this text and those are truth and love. Truth is the underlying virtue that I started with. I didn't make it part of our list because it is a part of the other virtues. Love closes this bookend as the virtue which encapsulates all others. While truth gives us a foundation for the other virtues mentioned, love supersedes all other virtues. Love covers all the virtues, while truth informs them. What this book is really telling you is how to love and how to build character so that you might be loving to everyone, including yourself. The term love is used in a flippant way in our society and it has been weakened by this usage. Loving others and ourselves is key to understanding ourselves and fulfilling our own purpose. The problem we have in society is that this "self-love" has been defined as selfishness. They call selfishness "self-love" in an attempt to allow bad behavior. Loving yourself does not mean being selfish. It is not all about you. Understanding the other virtues in this text gives us a better understanding of what it means to be kind and to love others and ourselves in a virtuous way.

10

Conclusion

T O RECAP, WE HAVE seen that building on truth we can live a
more fulfilled and successful life through the seven virtues I
have presented: humility, gratitude, diligence, agency, relationship,
forgiveness, and kindness (love). Let's just review a little bit. First,
all of these seven virtues are grounded in a bedrock of another
virtue: truth. Truth to oneself, truth before God, and truth with
those around us. What we might notice with all of these virtues
(though some more than others), is that they connect us to these
three relationships: God, others, and ourselves. Without truth, the
other virtues become a shadow of what they actually are. They become posturing before others. For example, we can pretend to be
humble, pretend to work hard, and pretend to be kind. Perhaps
that is better than outright contempt, but perhaps not. The point of
virtue is to work on oneself in order to live better and treat others
with respect. If we try to shortcut this process by not being honest
with ourselves, we will not actually do the work on our character
that makes this lasting change.

In addition, because these changes require changes in habit,
and habits that must continually be reinforced, it is worthless to
pretend because it is just a façade that is placed on top of rotten

character. Sooner or later your true self will come out, so you must change yourself to be the best self you can be through habit and virtue. Truth is the vehicle which allows you to do what must be done, because it will allow you to see the situation as it really is and point you to the actions that must be taken. Humility is ultimately embracing the truth about yourself. That is why false humility abounds. People misunderstand it to be the action of being lowly, but it is actually just being true to yourself and others. When you see that truth, it makes you humble, and that humility starts the process of these seven virtues.

Second, the backbone of this book arose from several years of personally engaging virtues as I tried to work on my own frustrations in life. Ultimately, the impetus to write the book as it currently stands comes from the pandemic of 2020 and 2021, but the core of it began much earlier. So, know that this text is rooted in approximately a decade of thinking about virtues. I still work toward the ideals I have presented in this text, but thus far, they have helped me greatly. A major reason I am writing this short text is so that my experience and the information of virtue for living is put in a concise way for me to review when I need it, and for my children to have when they are older. I hope it is helpful for you too. In addition, due to its setting in a tumultuous time, it also taught me the three things I discussed in chapter one: 1) *We must accept things that are out of our control.* 2) *We must be grateful for the things we do have,* and 3) *When faced with a new reality, expectations change, including relationship expectations.* Just as this text is the culmination of a long period of thought ignited by a catastrophic event, these three truths are timeless, and were refined by the events of the past year. Being able to speak the truth in your circumstances, first to yourself, and then to others, allows you to implement the virtues that you have been working on. These realities might point you to a path of virtue, or they might allow you to tap into the virtue you have already established. Basically, when things get tough you are directed to use your character to be loving to others, or you realize that you have work to do so that you can become the person you want to be. Of course this realization is on a spectrum. I don't think we are truly virtuous or totally lacking virtue in such a binary way. *Ideally*, we are all on the path to being more virtuous through our habits and our faith in God. My theology (and plenty of historical and personal experience) does not allow me to believe people become totally virtuous in this life. However, we can be a more virtuous person than we would be otherwise by implementing these core values.

The virtues presented in this book are not a magic pill. I strive for these all the time and fall short, but I know that they give a path to peace and productivity. The world has become a very stressful place, in part due to the acceleration of technology, as well as the eroding of virtue in family and public life. Technology is an accelerant for what is underneath, and what is underneath is a lack of virtue and a lack of trust in God. Perhaps in another text I can discuss the bastardization of Christianity in our modern world and how this twisted version of the truth has caused a lot of suffering in our society. When the Christian church fails in its mission, the ripples are felt in society. We are seeing that once again, as we have so many times in the past. But for now let's look at the two issues I mentioned that have contributed to the stressful situation we find ourselves in: technology and vice.

Technology is not bad. In fact, it can be a great thing. However, what it does do is magnify the problems and solutions we already have in a society. We have social networks that allow us to connect with people we had forgotten, and to network and create projects and organizations that would have difficulty existing otherwise. Social networks, smartphones, and basically all the tools built on the internet have allowed us to live a very "easy" life. That's a lot of power. They also destroy the fabric of our being by giving us a quick solution to long-term problems. We can create relationships and destroy them in a matter of seconds. Big Data has mined uncountable pieces of information, but that information can be used for good or evil. All this to say that we are living in a world that is very much outside our control, and this creates stress.[1] We are expected to do more, to do things a certain way, and to maintain empty relationships.

---

1. One paradox of this new reality is that our engagement with technology is more and more customizable, yet it separates us more from both ourselves

On the other hand, this is complimented by a lack of virtue, and outright vice, where people are not held accountable by others, and do not hold themselves accountable. Again, this is not a new problem. There is a reason we keep going back to ancient philosophy. The Greeks and Romans knew the problems of humanity (and often contributed to them). Their focus on virtue should be a hint to us. The early Christians built many of their systems of thought on the back of Greek philosophy, for good or ill, and this too, points us to solutions of virtue. We can dig into many other disparate philosophical systems and find virtue at their core. It's clear that virtue is a solution. When a society celebrates evil and vice, it becomes that much harder to be virtuous. What it does do, however, is point us to the one responsible for our actions: us. You are responsible for the way you act toward yourself and others. It may be easier sometimes than other times. It may be unfair that you have a steeper mountain to climb than the person next to you. It may be that you do not get what you "deserve." Basically, life isn't fair. Once you accept this, you are freed to work on your character, which will bring lasting change and success in your life. This will look differently for different people. You will not have total control; you never will. But you can control the things that you can control, and building up character and virtue are at the core of this. They are the engine that drives relationship and success. They are the foundation for your goals in life. And they must continually be strengthened through good habits.

There are a couple critiques I see arising from readers of this book. First, I don't tell you explicitly how to practice and build virtue. Second, I seem to create a balance of tension between what we can and cannot control. Let me address these two concerns so you don't leave this text with the feeling that you are missing something, or that there is any confusion.

To the first concern, that the book doesn't really talk about how to build virtue, I think that's a legitimate critique. Perhaps this is something that can be addressed in a future text. However, I really wanted to focus on the path of virtue and the virtues that are

---

and true relationship with others.

most important. The path includes emphases on each virtue, but there are different ways to achieve them. Take humility for example. The main action here is to set your mind to see yourself as you truly are in relation to others and God. This is going to look somewhat different for each person because your starting point will be different. There are many resources in print that can tell you how to work on humility, gratitude, and especially diligence and love. Some are better than others. What I'd like to get away from is a step-by-step approach to these virtues because each person *is* different. I also don't really have the desire to work on that at this time, partly because I think there are many self-professed gurus who are just saying the same things. Some of them have made their success by selling success, not actually achieving it. And I want the focus to be on the internal, virtuous path that will lead us to external action. This is one of the key messages contained in Christianity, as well as many other religions and philosophies. I want you to think as a result of reading this book, which then will lead to action. We want to focus on the internal self before moving outward.

Further, because this book is a set of meditations and ruminations on self and virtue, it is not meant to be a traditional self-help text. Set yourself right before God and others and let the actions emerge from this. Seek out other materials to support this as you have need, but just setting your mind right will bring you much peace, and peace can lead to success. If you are reading this, chances are you were already thinking about the types of issues I've been discussing. My goal is to share my experience. It takes discipline and focus, but by re-centering to these virtues, we are able to avoid some of the mental traps into which we fall. I continually struggle with them, but this cognitive process of virtue has been extremely helpful. Practically, I like to create lists and accomplish what is on those lists. They work better when they are tied to a schedule, because the structure helps you build habits to overcome your inclination to keep doing the same things over and over. This will take patience, but exercising these virtues in practice will make them easier. You may not make lists, but do find a way to be deliberate about building habits.

As for the second concern, those coming from a more Reformed Christian background (and maybe some Lutherans and Baptists), will have concerns about how I present agency. I believe this is a fundamental misunderstanding about the place of God's agency and human agency. All is in God's control. Unless you are a process theologian, God controls everything.[2] At the same time, we seemingly have free will. The misunderstanding comes from the place of appropriating the term "predestination" to all our actions, and not just the action of salvation through Jesus Christ (and if this doesn't interest you at all, just skip ahead a couple paragraphs—or learn something, it might be good for you!).

In an Augustinian view of sin, which Calvinists, Reformed, (and some) Lutherans and Baptists accept, humanity has sinned through Adam and Eve and because of this, everyone is guilty of sin. What this means is that we can no longer bring ourselves to God because God hates sin and humans are thus separated from the divine. This is ontological sin/guilt, as we discussed in chapter 8. Because of this, God must reach out to us and move us to Him. If this is the case, then we do not have free will in regard to our salvation (this will apply more to Reformed/Calvinists than many Lutherans/Baptists at this point—I could get really nuanced here, but let's save that for a theology text). If we no longer have free will in reference to this, then it stands we are predestined to salvation or not. This differs from God knowing what will happen, in which case we are free, but God has foreknowledge of future choices we will make. Where a lot of people go wrong, in my opinion, is that they apply this idea of predestination to every area of their life. Clearly you can make poor choices, and I'm fairly certain God is not making you do that.[3] So whether you decide to eat an extra hamburger, or choose to be diligent in your work day, that is in your

---

2. And even for those who don't believe God controls everything, the objective reality is that He does or does not. It's not an open question from an objective standpoint. I believe He does based theological argumentation, history, Scripture, and personal experience.

3. There may be debatable exceptions, such as the pharaoh narrative in the book of Exodus, but in general God would not have you sin. Yes, this is a whole other can of worms.

control. Sometimes you might need some spiritual help, but you can choose to do what is right through the power of the Holy Spirit.

That said, I think the critique that we cannot control anything is wrong, as there are things we can control and things we cannot. We should try to change the things we can when necessary. Sometimes things are out of our control because the world is bigger than us, and sometimes because of spiritual reasons. What I am advocating for in this book is to take control of the things you can control, and through the power of God decide and execute those things to the best of your ability.

Let me finish by reiterating that by instituting the seven virtues in these three categories we can live a more successful, meaningful life: Attitude→Humility/Gratitude | Action→Diligence/Agency | Agreement→Relationship/Forgiveness/Kindness-Love. By doing this we will strengthen our character, our productivity, and peace in our lives. By strengthening our own lives, we will influence and strengthen the lives of others to build a stronger community. Virtue and behavior can be forced in a top-down manner, and that can be successful, but it is much less successful than in a bottom-up approach, where people are stronger and more virtuous through building up their character. So instead of trying to make weak people behave (top-down), strong people are going to do what comes naturally, and that is exude good character (bottom-up).

Go ahead and take this step. It may take a long while, or it may tap into behaviors and attitudes already present in your life that need revitalizing. You cannot go wrong in choosing good character and virtue. It will not only make you better, but also those around you. You will find that the time you lack to do things may suddenly appear, and the goals you chase may come more into view. In other cases you might find those previous goals aren't worth pursuing. Choose virtue. Choose success. Submit to God and the good in life. The pleasures you now enjoy will be replaced by something far greater. Why clutch tightly to a piece of copper, when there are diamonds there for the taking?

Bibliography

Aristotle. *Nicomachean Ethics*. Rev. ed. Edited by Roger Crisp. Cambridge Texts in the History of Philosophy. Cambridge: Cambridge University Press, 2014.

Bondi, Roberta C. *To Love as God Loves*. Philadelphia: Fortress, 1987.

Evagrius Ponticus. *Evagrius of Pontus: The Greek Ascetic Corpus*. Edited by Robert E. Sinkewicz. Oxford Early Christian Studies. New York: Oxford University Press, 2003.

Hadot, Pierre. *Philosophy as a Way of Life: Spiritual Exercises from Socrates to Foucault*. Edited by Arnold I. Davidson. Translated by Michael Chase. Oxford: Blackwell, 1995.

The Holy Bible. New Revised Standard Version. New York: Oxford University Press, 1989.

"Ontological." *Merriam-Webster Dictionary*. https://www.merriam-webster.com/dictionary/ontological.

"Read Your Bible, Pray Every Day." *Children's Bible Songs*. https://childrensbiblesongs.us/2011/09/read-your-bible-pray-every-day/.

"Social Networking and Ethics." *Stanford Encyclopedia of Philosophy*, August 3, 2012. https://plato.stanford.edu/entries/ethics-social-networking/.

Tsakiridis, George. *Evagrius Ponticus and Cognitive Science: A Look at Moral Evil and the Thoughts*. Eugene, OR: Pickwick, 2010.

———. "Habit as a Spiritual Discipline in Early Christianity." In *Habits in Mind: Integrating Theology, Philosophy, and the Cognitive Science of Virtue, Emotion and Character Formation*, edited by Gregory R. Peterson, et al., 77–88. Philosophical Studies of Science and Religion. Leiden: Brill, 2017.

www.ingramcontent.com/pod-product-compliance
Lightning Source LLC
Chambersburg PA
CBHW060423090426
42734CB00011B/2423